Jean-Pierre Jeunet |

03496

This book is due for return on or before the last date shown below.

2 0 OCT 2011

0 9 MAR 2012

Contemporary Film Directors

Edited by James Naremore

The Contemporary Film Directors series provides concise, well-written introductions to directors from around the world and from every level of the film industry. Its chief aims are to broaden our awareness of important artists, to give serious critical attention to their work, and to illustrate the variety and vitality of contemporary cinema. Contributors to the series include an array of internationally respected critics and academics. Each volume contains an incisive critical commentary, an informative interview with the director, and a detailed filmography.

A list of books in the series appears at the end of this book.

Jean-Pierre Jeunet |

Elizabeth Ezra

UNIVERSITY
OF
ILLINOIS
PRESS
URBANA
AND
CHICAGO

Library of Congress Cataloging-in-Publication Data
Ezra, Elizabeth
Jean-Pierre Jeunet / Elizabeth Ezra.
p. cm. — (Contemporary film directors)
Includes bibliographical references and index.
ISBN-13 978-0-252-03318-6 (cloth : alk. paper)
ISBN-10 0-252-03318-3 (cloth : alk. paper)
ISBN-13 978-0-252-07522-3 (pbk. : alk. paper)
ISBN-10 0-252-07522-6 (cloth : alk. paper)
1. Jeunet, Jean-Pierre, 1955—Criticism and interpretation.
I. Title.
PN1998.3.J47E97   2008
791.4302'33092—dc22   2007037071

To Simon, who has yet to see a film,
and Nathan, who has seen a few.

Contents |

Preface and Acknowledgments |

The prevailing trend among film scholars has been to view Jean-Pierre Jeunet's work with a certain amount of disdain, claiming that it is too slick, too heavily influenced by advertising aesthetics, and too sentimental—in short, too popular, but not populist enough. Distinguished colleagues, mentors, and friends of mine dismiss Jeunet for being too theatrical and not spontaneous enough—in other words, for not being Jean-Luc Godard, Agnès Varda, or François Truffaut. But today, slick is the new populism: the revolutionary spontaneity of May 1968 has transmogrified into flash mob happenings meticulously orchestrated by text messaging, podcasts, and blogs that, like the best art, appear deceptively spontaneous to spectators and bystanders. As theatrical and minutely planned as Jeunet's films are, they show us what populism looks like today: advertising, music videos, and computer games. The energy that Jeunet's films tap into is as high-voltage as the energy that fueled the French New Wave. The new digital and computer graphics–based technologies embraced by Jeunet and his collaborators are similar in impact to the (at the time, equally new) technologies of handheld cameras and high-sensitivity film stock that allowed Godard and Truffaut to take to the streets to make their films. In the 1990s and 2000s, however, the streets have become clogged with cars whose drivers are sealed off from the world through which they glide. To be fresh and innovative is no longer only a question of going outward but of turning inward as well, to the real and virtual worlds of memory, history, and desire. And it is to these worlds that Jeunet has gone and to which he returns with each new film.

This study of Jeunet's work was made possible by funding for teaching assistance from the Faculty of Arts at the University of Stirling and by a research grant from the Carnegie Trust of Scotland, for which I am very grateful. I wish to thank those conference and seminar organizers who invited me to present portions of this research at the Universities of Amsterdam, Edinburgh, London, Miami, Nottingham, Stirling, and Swansea. I also wish to thank Cherise Saywell for her advice and friendly support, Matthew Mitchell for his excellent copyediting, and my students at Stirling, especially Martyn Burrow and Deborah McKenzie, whose insights were always illuminating. I am grateful to Alison Cooper once again for her knowledge, competence, and unfailing patience, and to my colleagues Alison Jasper and Andrew Hass for their help in deciphering the religious allusions in *Alien Resurrection.* I also wish to thank Jean-Pierre Jeunet for allowing me to translate and publish a portion of his commentary from *Auto/Focus,* and Charlotte Janos of KM Productions and Marjorie at Tapioca Films for their assistance. Small portions of this book were originally published, in different form, in *New Cinemas* 1.1 (November 2001) and *French Cultural Studies* 15.3 (October 2004). Finally, thanks as ever to Paul Jackson and, more recently, Nathan and Simon, for providing what seemed like happy distraction, but which was really at the heart of everything.

Prosthetic Visions |

Jean-Pierre Jeunet is that rare breed, a popular auteur. He has written or cowritten all but one of the screenplays for the films he has directed and has maintained a high degree of creative control over his projects, which bear his distinctive stylistic stamp and have been generally well regarded by critics. At the same time, his films have attracted increasingly large audiences, with accordingly expanding budgets. Yet his success is also his Achilles' heel: his popularity with audiences has tended to marginalize him among film scholars and academics, some of whom regard his films with suspicion. Critics have dismissed Jeunet for what they see as his privileging of form over content. Yet this form itself contains a great deal of substance. Jeunet's films are historically resonant in their association with the late twentieth-century French film style known as the *cinéma du look* and in their persistent allusions—even within films set in a postapocalyptic future, which nonetheless manage to look like costume dramas—to earlier film movements such as German expressionism, French poetic realism, and the French New Wave.

Jeunet's films thematize issues such as the technological mediation of social relations, cultural anxieties surrounding advances in biotechnology, and the repression and subsequent revelation of historical trauma, especially in the context of war and decolonization. Looking to the past and the future, his films invariably express the millennial anxieties and preoccupations of the present.

Jeunet's work also exemplifies the expanding transnational dimension of French cinema not only by virtue of the global box-office success of his films but also because of the director's increasing engagement with Hollywood. Jeunet's first feature film, *Delicatessen* (1991), codirected with Marc Caro, made an impression among film buffs and developed a cult status outside of France, but it was not a blockbuster. *La Cité des enfants perdus* (The city of lost children; 1995), the second (and, to date, the last) film Jeunet made with Caro, initially remained obscure outside of France (though its cult following grew steadily in the first years of the 2000s), but its international credentials were established by virtue of its American lead actor, Ron Perlman, who played the role with heavily accented French. Soon thereafter, Jeunet went to Hollywood to make *Alien Resurrection* (1997), bringing with him some of the French technicians and actors with whom he had begun to form a company of sorts. Jeunet then returned to France to make *Le Fabuleux destin d'Amélie Poulain* (*Amélie*, 2001), a relatively small-scale French film that was an enormous domestic and international success and that, much more than the big-budget *Alien Resurrection*, put Jeunet's name on the global cinematic map. His next film, *Un Long dimanche de fiançailles* (A very long engagement; 2004), despite being shot in France, in French, with a virtually all-French cast and crew (though it did feature an extended cameo by the Hollywood star Jodie Foster), was the subject of a protracted legal battle to determine whether the film, which was partly financed by the French arm of Warner Brothers, was "French" enough to receive state subsidies. For his next film, *The Life of Pi* (still in production as this book went to press), which he made after turning down an offer to make the fourth *Harry Potter* film, Jeunet literally and figuratively returned to Hollywood.

Jeunet never attended film school; he is entirely self-taught. Born in 1953 in Roanne, he came from a modest background. His father worked for the phone company, and his mother was a schoolteacher. He began making animated films while working for the telephone company and then graduated to filmed advertisements and music videos. Jeunet's career has been defined by a series of collaborative partnerships, some more long-standing than others. Of these working relationships, perhaps the most influential was his collaboration with the illustrator and graphic artist Marc Caro. Jeunet met Caro at an animation festival in Annecy in the 1970s, and the pair clicked right away. They made two short animated puppet films together, *L'évasion* (The escape; 1978) and *Le manège* (The carousel; 1979), before going on to make two more short films in the 1980s, *Le Bunker de la dernière rafale* (The bunker of the last gunshots; 1981) and *Pas de repos pour Billy Brakko* (No rest for Billy Brakko; 1983). Marc Caro has described the way in which he and Jeunet complement each other: "[Jeunet] loves Charlie Chaplin, whereas I love Buster Keaton; he loves Truffaut, while I love Jacques Tati; he likes dogs, and I like cats. What we have most in common is the love of *making* things. It's true that we had this desire, more than anything else, to *make* a film, rather than simply to help another director or filmmaker" (Drubigny).

The pair's feature debut, *Delicatessen,* launched both their careers, and their second feature-length film, the visually opulent *Cité des enfants perdus,* solidified their reputation as filmmakers with a strong visual aesthetic, a predilection for dystopian fantasy, and an off-kilter sense of humor. Both films credited Jeunet and Caro as codirectors, and the filmmakers worked in tandem, with Caro taking more responsibility for the films' visual style and Jeunet working more with the actors. Caro has explained their working relationship thus: "Jean-Pierre handles the direction in the traditional sense of the word, that is, the direction of the actors, etc., while I do the artistic direction. Beyond that, in the day-to-day workings of the shoot or preproduction, it's obviously much more of a mixture. We write together, film together, edit together. According to each of our specialties, sometimes we'll be drawn to what we do best. There's a real complicity between us" (Debemardi).

This almost symbiotic partnership—like that of the conjoined twins in *La Cité des enfants perdus,* who finish each other's sentences and scratch each other's arms—came to an end when Jeunet and Caro were offered the chance to direct the fourth *Alien* film. Caro was not interested in working on a film over which he lacked creative control, whereas

Jeunet relished the challenges and constraints that come with working on a big-budget Hollywood movie. Although Caro was eventually persuaded to spend three weeks in Hollywood doing some costume and set design for the film, he then parted company with Jeunet to pursue a solo career in illustration and computer graphics. Caro subsequently declined to participate in any of the "making-of" documentaries or interviews to accompany the DVD editions of the pair's films, and the two have not worked together since. This parting of ways could perhaps have been foreseen in their differing responses when asked, in a joint interview, "Cinematically, what are your aspirations?" Caro replied, "I feel I'd like to explore other narrative forms, ones in which there's a little media interactivity. What especially interests me is developing universes, and multimedia can enable me to explore a universe that I will construct." Jeunet responded somewhat differently: "I'd like to continue writing screenplays . . . something like *Forrest Gump*, where the special effects aren't necessarily seen but can enable things to be done that couldn't have been, previously . . . in turn, reviving the writing, in proposing new things, thanks to the new techniques" (Schlockoff and Karani).

Other members of Jeunet's coterie have maintained closer ties with the director. The producer Claudie Ossard, who helped Jeunet and Caro finance *Delicatessen,* stayed with Jeunet throughout the next decade of his career, producing his two subsequent French films. Pierre-Jacques Bénichou has worked as casting director on all Jeunet's films except for *Alien Resurrection,* when there was a Hollywood casting director in place. The special-effects supervisor Pitof, who has worked on several of Jeunet's films, and the director of photography Darius Khondji, who had worked on *Delicatessen* and *La Cité des enfants perdus,* went with Jeunet to Hollywood to work on *Alien Resurrection.* The set designer Jean Rabasse and the set decorator Aline Bonetto have worked on all of Jeunet's French films, as have the screenwriters Guillaume Laurant and Gilles Adrian. Bruno Delbonnel has worked on all of Jeunet's films in several different roles, from screenwriter and sound technician to director of photography. Several actors have appeared in more than one of Jeunet's films, including the late Ticky Holgado, Serge Merlin, Rufus, Ron Perlman, Jean-Claude Dreyfus, Audrey Tautou, and Dominique Bettenfeld. Dominique Pinon has acted in all of the director's feature films as well as the short film *Foutaises* (Trifles; 1990).

Jeunet has been at the cutting edge of French cinema's use of computer-generated images (CGI) and digital technology to produce special effects. At the time of its release in 1995, *La Cité des enfants perdus* could boast the greatest number of digital effects of any French film ever made. Marc Caro has recalled working on that film and the sea change that the advent of digital technology made possible: "We came from the world of animation, where you're used to doing everything image by image. . . . And then, digital technology came along and turned everything upside down, and hit us over the head, but at the same time, we were partly responsible for it, actively participating in the innovation—it's really fascinating. You sort of get that feeling of pride that 'pioneers' sometimes have" (Drubigny). When Jeunet went on to release *Amélie* in France in 2001, it was the film's use of digital technology to transform Paris into an idealized version of itself that attracted the most attention. Digital technology allowed Jeunet both to film on location and to transform his locations into an enormous set. This blend of authenticity and artifice evokes aspects of the 1980s and 1990s *cinéma du look*, the late 1950s and early 1960s French New Wave, and the big-budget, postwar *cinéma de qualité*. What is distinctive about Jeunet's films is the way they combine the past and the present to create a style that is discernible across all his films, even the two he made with Marc Caro. Jeunet's trademarks include a quirky sense of humor; characters who exhibit slightly neurotic, ritualistic behavior or "magical thinking" (especially Amélie and Mathilde in *Amélie* and *Un Long dimanche de fiançailles*, respectively); obsessive collections (the narrator's cousin in *Foutaises;* the diver in *La Cité des enfants perdus;* Nino in *Amélie*); and a preoccupation with feet (the large number of shots at ground level—and therefore of feet—in all of Jeunet's feature films; the emphasis on the distinction between Louison's enormous clown shoes and Julie's tiny shoes in *Delicatessen;* Miette and One's discussion in *La Cité des enfants perdus* in which shoes are used as a metaphor for conjugal union). Jeunet is renowned for his meticulous preparation and storyboarding, and his films have sometimes come under attack for a perceived lack of spontaneity. He has claimed, however, that he is not wedded to his storyboard: "'I'm the first to say that a storyboard isn't made to be respected but to be transcended. If an actor finds a brilliant idea or if you think of a way of shooting the same thing differently and better, then you have to change everything, no doubt about it. In other words, the storyboard is like a highway: you can turn off it from time to time to follow prettier country roads, but if you lose your way, you can always return to the highway'" (qtd. in Tirard 116).

The high degree of advance preparation, the emphasis on visual style, and the obvious influence of advertising and music-video aesthetics underscore Jeunet's loose affiliation with the films and filmmakers of the *cinéma du look*. The *cinéma du look* emerged in the early 1980s, beginning with *Diva* (dir. Jean-Jacques Beineix; 1981), a cult film hailed by Fredric Jameson as the first "postmodern" French film (Jameson 55–62) that soon became the signature film of the *look* style. The directors most closely associated with the *cinéma du look* are Beineix, Luc Besson, and Léos Carax, who made a number of stylish thrillers characterized by sleek, colorful urban settings, a high degree of artifice, and what Sue Harris has called "a celebration of the visual and sensory elements of the filmic text" (Harris, "Cinéma" 219). The influence of commercials and pop-music videos can be seen in virtually every frame of *look* films such as Beineix's *Lune dans le caniveau* (The moon in the gutter; 1983) and *37,2 le matin* (Betty blue; 1986); Besson's *Subway* (1985), *Nikita* (La femme Nikita; 1990), and *The Fifth Element* (1997); and Carax's *Boy Meets Girl* (1984), *Mauvais Sang* (Bad blood; 1986), *Les Amants du Pont-neuf* (The Lovers on the bridge; 1991), and *Pola X* (1999). In these films, critics often commented, plot and character development seemed to be little more than pretexts for the dazzling visual display. In his study of Beineix, Phil Powrie describes the *look* effect as "the immersion of the spectator, not in some kind of 'depth' but paradoxically, in an infinite 'surface.' That surface is seen as the screen surface: the spectator does not go beyond the surface of the narrative, which functions more like a peg on which to hang the coat of style. The spectator does not go beyond the surface of the character, because it is not the psychological complexity of the character which gives pleasure, but the way in which the character behaves. In other words, what matters is what can be seen, what is presented, rather than what can be worked out, or constructed" (Powrie, *Jean-Jacques Beineix* 15). The emphasis on what can be seen also results in a fascination with technologies of vision and visual representation, especially in *Amélie* (telescopes and binoculars but also photography, painting, postcards, video, television, and cinema) and *Un Long dimanche de fiançailles* (in which point-of-view shots through microscopes, magnifying glasses, cameras, and the viewfinders of machine guns proliferate). Jeunet's films offer a tremendous degree of surface pleasure, but what makes them so interesting for the film analyst is their imaginative use of the surface or "look" of the films as a vehicle with which to conceal and convey a great deal of information about contemporary cultural preoccupations, which, like Edgar Allen Poe's purloined letter, can be hidden in plain sight.

Jeunet rose to prominence in the 1990s, when the *cinéma du look* had fallen out of favor, to be replaced by the social preoccupations of the *cinéma de banlieue* (emblematized by Mathieu Kassovitz's *La Haine;* 1995) and the new realist aesthetic exemplified by such films as Sandrine Veysset's *Y aura-t-il de la neige à noël?* (Will it snow for Christmas?; 1996), Bruno Dumont's *La Vie de Jésus* (The life of Jesus; 1997) and *L'Humanitié* (Humanity; 1999), Eric Zonca's *La Vie rêvée des anges* (The dreamlife of angels; 1998), and Robert Guédiguian's *Marius et Jeannette* (1999). Jeunet's background in advertising and music videos naturally predisposed him to the *look* aesthetic (or perhaps it was his *look* sensibility that first attracted him to advertising and music videos). There are incidental overlaps between Jeunet's work and that of other *look* films, such as the presence of Dominique Pinon (who memorably played a smalltime thug in *Diva*) and the use of a location from *Nikita* for the exterior shots in *Delicatessen*. But there are also more fundamental overlaps, such as a shared emphasis on visual appeal, the extensive use of caricature, and repeated allusions to past film styles.

Jeunet's invocation of a number of different eras in film history is one aspect of his collage aesthetic. This aesthetic is dramatized in the emphasis on reconstruction in Jeunet's films—in its most extended narrative form in *Un Long dimanche de fiançailles,* in which Mathilde must piece together fragments of accounts of the war; but also in *Alien Resurrection,* when scientists reconstruct Ripley from fragments of "genetic material" found by her human predecessor's remains; in *Amélie,* when Amélie cuts and pastes sentences to form a phony letter from her concierge's dead husband, or when Nino must reassemble fragments of a torn photo to make out Amélie's message about meeting up, or when Amélie forces Nino to "read" the series of photos of Amélie's body parts like a rebus to learn of her desire to meet him. The collage aesthetic stems from

Jeunet's early work with Caro (*Billy Brakko* in particular) and develops in subsequent works, in which it takes two forms. The first form is the literal assemblage of fragments into a coherent whole in either a single frame (as in *Billy Brakko,* when we see various cartoon characters as well as a photograph of Marc Caro's head pasted next to each other) or in a montage sequence (in *Foutaises, Amélie,* and *Un Long dimanche de fiançailles*). The second, more general form taken by Jeunet's collage aesthetic is the mixing of media and genres from disparate sources. The collage aesthetic has its roots in surrealism but goes back in the French tradition at least as far as Michel de Montaigne, whose essays juxtaposed citations from a seemingly endless array of sources.

Jeunet's frame of reference, like that of all filmmakers, is constructed from a wide range of cultural influences. In Jeunet's case these influences are often unabashedly popular, including the work of the animator Tex Avery (the creator of the cartoon characters Porky Pig and Daffy Duck), the television series "Mission: Impossible," the Spaghetti Westerns of Sergio Leone, and the films of Jacques Audiard, whom Jeunet cites as his favorite contemporary director (Drubigny). Jeunet was also profoundly influenced by older cultural icons such as Jules Verne, the first and best-loved French science-fiction writer of the modern era; the poetic realist filmmakers Jacques Prévert and Marcel Carné; and Federico Fellini, whose films depicting the oneiric underworld of the circus are evoked in *Delicatessen* and *La Cité des enfants perdus.* Related to the collage aesthetic is Jeunet's penchant for elaborate, Rube Goldberg–like chain reactions, suggesting an interconnectedness among the vast array of human endeavor. Through editing, Jeunet emphasizes connections that would not otherwise be apparent. In what has become the most famous sequence of *Delicatessen,* the activities of cello practice, carpet beating, wall painting, toy making, and bicycle pumping all fall into step with the rhythms of the butcher's lovemaking. In *La Cité des enfants perdus,* a teardrop triggers a series of events that culminates in the collision of a huge ship into a pier. And in *Amélie,* the disparate activities occurring at the moment of Amélie's conception—the beating of a fly's wings, the dance of glasses on a windswept tablecloth in an outdoor café, the death of a friend—are cataloged, giving the impression that they are linked on some world-historical level. At the end of *Amélie,* when we are told that there are more connections in the human brain than there are molecules in the universe, it is not difficult to believe, because we have seen this assertion demonstrated in the film.

The cinema of the fantastic is another tradition whose influence on Jeunet's work is important to note. Like the *cinéma du look*, it has been marginalized by critics because of its popular appeal. The French tradition of the cinema of the fantastic, or the *cinéma fantastique*, has its roots in the work of Georges Méliès, a magician and entrepreneur whose pioneering film career lasted from 1896 to 1913. He became known for his fantasy and "trick" films, which showed off Méliès's prowess as a magician and the new medium's capacity for illusion and special effects. Since the days of Méliès, there has been a distinctive tradition of the fantastic in French cinema, from the Feuillade serial *Les Vampires*, to surrealism, to the whimsical science-fiction and fantasy films of René Clair (*Paris qui dort, Le Fantôme du Moulin-Rouge, Le Voyage imaginaire, Les Belles de nuit*), to Jean Cocteau (*La Belle et la Bête, Le Sang d'un Poète, Orphée*), Jacques Tourneur (*The Cat People*), Georges Franju (*Les Yeux sans visage*), Jean-Luc Godard (*Alphaville*), François Truffaut (*Fahrenheit 451*), Jean-Marie Poiré (*Les Visiteurs*), and Luc Besson (*The Fifth Element*).

This tradition has been largely ignored by critics and film scholars, who tend to focus on the Anglo-U.S. cinema of the fantastic. French filmmakers wanting to make fantasy films have often ended up going to Britain or the United States and making their films in English (as the number of English titles in the list above attests). Jeunet has commented on this lack of sympathy toward the fantastic in France: "In literature, we think about and accept the fantastical style all the time, but in film, that's not always the case, especially in France. Sometimes they hate the style. They prefer ugly things, realistic movies. I love to play with everything: the sound, the costumes, the camera" (Tobias). To a large extent, this lack of critical recognition can be attributed to the artificial division between fantasy and realist film. From the beginning, film historians have, rather simplistically, opposed the work of Méliès to the more realistic films of the Lumière brothers, whose *actualités*, or proto-newsreels and slice-of-life scenes, came to be associated with the more critically esteemed realist and naturalist genres. But just as the Lumières' films display evidence of constructed, non-naturalistic design, Méliès's work is far from exclusively fantastical (see Ezra, *Georges Méliès* chap. 2). Like Méliès, Jeunet sets out to amaze and delight viewers, but his films are not pure flights of fancy. They deal with issues of cultural and historical importance and, most persistently, with the cultural status and function of history. Jeunet's films depict the severing of ties with the past and its prosthetic restoration through the medium of film itself and through other mediatic representations.

One way that Jeunet's films figure the severing of ties with the past is through the image of the orphan. Anyone who has seen at least a couple of Jeunet's feature films will have been struck by the preoponderance of parentless (or at least motherless) girls and young women who feature in them. Long before Jeunet found his muse in Audrey Tautou, his films tended to feature waiflike female characters who inhabited a cinematic city of lost children. In *Delicatessen,* the butcher's daughter Julie is alienated from her murderous father, and there is no mention of Julie's mother. In *La Cité des enfants perdus,* the band of kidnapped children used as guinea pigs in a mad scientist's experiments are, to all intents and purposes, orphans; as they sail off at the end of the film, presumably to form a makeshift family, there is no mention of their biological parents. The large assortment of clones in the film are also lost children, the biotechnological products of a single man. In *Alien Resurrection,* Ripley is a clone, and an absent mother is suggested at the outset in the voiceover that accompanies the image of the adolescent Ripley developing in a vat of liquid: "My mommy always told me there were no monsters; no real ones. But there are." The identity of the "mommy" is ambiguous; it could refer either to the "original" Ripley from two hundred years earlier, from whose DNA this Ripley was cloned, or it could invoke Ripley's status as a surrogate mother to the little girl whom she took under her wing in the second film in the *Alien* quartet, *Aliens* (dir. James Cameron; 1986), whose exact words she now repeats. The little girl's death in the earlier film would position Ripley as a forever "absent" mother, with the guilt that accompanies the feeling that she failed to protect the child. In *Amélie* and *Un Long dimanche de fiançailles,* one or both parents are killed in freak accidents: Amélie's mother is crushed to death by a suicidal Québecois tourist plunging from the top of the Notre Dame Cathedral, while Mathilde's parents, we are told, were killed in a tram accident (in a departure from the novel on which the film is based). The protagonist of Jeunet's sixth feature film, *Life of Pi*, is a boy whose parents are killed in a shipwreck.

Biological reproduction, in other words, is essentially elided in Jeunet's films. The desire to banish all thoughts of it is expressed in the short film *Foutaises* in the wish to dissociate sex from the knowledge of female anatomy: when "making love with a woman," the narrator tells us, he doesn't like thinking about "what's inside," as we are shown anatomical diagrams of the female reproductive system. In a similar moment in *Amélie*, we are told of Georgette's dislike for the expression "the fruit of thy womb," with an insert of an anatomical chart depicting the female reproductive organs. The only exception to the otherwise widespread elision of biological reproduction occurs in the precredit opening sequence of *Amélie*, which shows Amélie's conception, complete with sperm and egg uniting under a miscroscope and time-lapse photography showing the progressively developing pregnancy of Amélie's mother—this sequence could be a tongue-in-cheek allusion to the lack of biological parents elsewhere in Jeunet's films. Amélie's ancestral connection to the past, however, is soon truncated, as her mother is quickly dispensed with by the suicidal Québecois tourist. Amélie's father is completely ineffectual, showing his daughter little affection as a child and offering her little in the way of emotional support when she becomes an adult. The only other living father in Jeunet's films, the butcher in *Delicatessen*, has a similarly strained relationship (to say the least) with his daughter. Parenthood in Jeunet's films is represented almost exclusively in surrogate form, as in *Un Long dimanche de fiançailles*, when the mother of a soldier killed in the war "adopts" Manech as her own under false pretenses, and when Mathilde's aunt and uncle stand in for her deceased mother and father. In *La Cité des enfants perdus*, the conjoined twins act as mother-substitutes to the children in their care, though more in the wicked-stepmother mold, as they exploit the children for financial gain rather than nurturing them.

The figure of the orphan is standard in children's literature (*Harry Potter* is a recent example) and in the fairy-tale genre in particular. This genre is invoked explicitly in *La Cité des enfants perdus* in the tale of the "wicked genetic fairy" as well as in the cameo appearance by Nane Germon, who played one of Beauty's wicked stepsisters in Jean

Cocteau's *La Belle et la bête*. All the parentless characters in Jeunet's films represent severed links with the past. Jeunet's films return almost obsessively—and often anachronistically—to the past, whether through production design and costumes or in the privileging of outmoded entertainment forms such as the circus (*Delicatessen* and *La Cité des enfants perdus*), newsreels (*Amélie, Un Long dimanche de fiançailles*), and early television (*Delicatessen, Amélie*). In *Alien Resurrection*, even though the film is set in the future, the production design evokes earlier eras in its color palette, costumes, and sets. It was not until *Un Long dimanche de fiançailles* that Jeunet set a film explicitly in the past.

While *cinéma du look* films allude to past movements in film history, Jeunet's films go beyond allusion, engaging with past eras and film movements in ways that, though at times enigmatic, form an essential part of the films' overall effect. Film movements invoked frequently include German expressionism (notably in *Le Manège, Le Bunker de la dernière rafale*, and *La Cité des enfants perdus*) and the French New Wave (*Amélie* and, to some extent, *Un Long dimanche de fiançailles*), but above all, it is French poetic realism whose influence is felt most forcefully, and most fondly, in Jeunet's films. From the 1930s-era gangster allusions and film-noir car-chase sequence in *Billy Brakko*, to the clips from Jean Gabin movies in *Foutaises*, to the Second Empire cobblestoned courtyards of *Delicatessen* and *Amélie*, and the seedy dockside setting of *La Cité des enfants perdus*, Jeunet's films often invoke with some nostalgia the communal ethos of the Popular Front era, with its attendant empowerment of *le peuple*, or working men and women of modest means, who rebel against their oppressors. In *Delicatessen*, inhabitants of the apartment building, led by a janitor and former circus clown, rise up and overthrow the evil butcher who has been controlling their lives. In *La Cité des enfants perdus*, a sailor and a band of ragtag children elude the clutches of a mad scientist. In *Alien Resurrection*, a motley crew of spaceship technicians, rebellious robots, and unruly clones overcome corporate and military domination along with the space aliens. (In a line cut from the theatrical release of the film but included in the 2003 special edition DVD, Ripley is informed that the "Corporation," her previous incarnation's nemesis two hundred years earlier, has been bought out by Wal-Mart.) In *Amélie*, a young waitress's matchmaking schemes and varied attempts to brighten the lives of her working-class neighbors and coworkers invariably result in the triumph of the underdog in the face of loneliness or social exclusion. And in *Un Long dimanche de fiançailles,* Mathilde stands up to the military's wall of silence about the death of her lighthouse-keeper fiancé: although Mathilde comes from a reasonably well-to-do background and so does not qualify as one of *le peuple,* her independent spirit and challenge to authority evoke Popular Front cinema—with the significant difference that, in Jeunet's films, the shows of defiance are successful, which is rarely the case in poetic realism (see Andrew, *Mists of Regret* 49).

These links to the past, however, are above all conveyed in the films' visual style—in the costumes, hairstyles, props, and lighting, but especially the sets. In *Delicatessen,* the cobblestoned courtyard and Second Empire apartment dwelling, with its final rooftop scene, evokes poetic realist films such as *Le Jour se lève* (Daybreak; dir. Marcel Carné, 1939), *Sous les toits de Paris* (Beneath the rooftops of Paris; dir. René Clair, 1930), and *Le Crime de Monsieur Lange* (The crime of Monsieur Lange; dir. Jean Renoir, 1936), while in *Cité,* the misty harbor and narrow alleyways of the port town evoke films such as *Le Quai des brumes* (Port of shadows; dir. Marcel Carné, 1938) and *Pépé le Moko* (dir. Julien Duvivier; 1937). Jeunet tends to favor what Charles Affron and Mirella Affron designate as "the artificial set" or "decor of artifice," set designs that serve as "a primary focus of the narrative, challenging the force of plot and character. The viewer exits the theatre whistling the sets" (Affron and Affron 39). Such decor, they argue, "has the privilege to create new realities, contexts apt for the monstrous and the uncanny, dream worlds conjured out of the fantastic, projective visions of the future" (39). Ironically, even Jeunet's visions of the future (in *Delicatessen, Cité,* and *Alien Resurrection*), as well as those of the present (*Amélie*), look much like the past. In these films, history is flattened out onto the film set, as though the past whose severing is represented by the lost generation of parents were trying to find a way back in. That the past seeping into the present is often the period surrounding the Second World War is not surprising, considering that the 1990s was a period of national soul-searching in France, as the extent of the country's complicity in the crimes of the war became apparent through the highly publicized trials of the war criminals Klaus Barbie and Maurice Papon.

In the films that thematize cloning (*La Cité des enfants perdus* and *Alien Resurrection*), there is an added dimension to this tension between present and past in the suggestion of a collapse of the diachrony of generations. With cloning, there is no sense of a reproductive life cycle and the succession of filiation through time. This flattening out of generations is emblematized by the hint of Oedipal emotional entanglements, for example, in the multiple familial and romantic roles that Miette and her adult protector One fulfill for one another: he is variously invoked as her father, her brother, and her lover. Similarly, Krank and his entourage, who are all cloned contemporaries and thus technically siblings, are alternately referred to as mother and children (Marthe and the identical clones), husband and wife (Krank and Marthe), and brothers (Krank and the identical clones). In *Alien Resurrection,* there is a strong hint of a sexual liaison between Ripley and her alien grandchild.

Above all, though, the severing of the past is symbolized by the recurring motif of mutilation—the source of the trauma that, both etymologically and symbolically, is the result of a wounding. As early as *Le Bunker de la dernière rafale,* amputation is signaled by the presence of prosthetic limbs that the military scientists use for their human experiments. In the feature films, the motif of mutilation is foregrounded rather starkly, first in *Delicatessen,* in the occupation of the butcher and in his extracurricular activities. And dismemberment drives the plot of *Un Long dimanche de fiançailles,* as five soldiers are condemned to die for committing self-mutilation in order to be sent home. In between these two films, mutilation and bodily disintegration or infirmity are figured in incidental or peripheral contexts, but with noteworthy frequency: the disembodied brain in *La Cité des enfants perdus* and the self-blinded Cyclops cult members; the caesarian section performed on Ripley in *Alien Resurrection,* the gaping bullet wound in Call's abdomen, assorted alien "chest-burst" parturition scenes, and Vriess's wheelchair; Lucien the grocery clerk's withered arm in *Amélie,* Mademoiselle Suzanne's limp, the Glass Man's infirmity, and the one-legged tap dancer in the video compilation Amélie gives him; Mathilde's polio-induced limp, Petit Louis's artificial hand, and an assortment of other instances of mutilation in *Un Long dimanche de fiançailles.* At a self-referential level, this preoccupation with bodily disintegration could point to a desire for cinematic wholeness, a nostalgia for an idealized period in film history. But on a more general level, these images symbolize a cutting off of the past and, in particular, of unpleasant historical events.

Memory plays a complex role in Jeunet's films, which enact both its repression and its return. In *La Cité des enfants perdus*, for example, the creator of the clones suffers from amnesia and only regains his memory at the moment of his death. Amélie's first good deed is to rekindle the childhood memories of a former inhabitant of her apartment. And *Un Long dimanche de fiançailles* is about a woman's attempt to reconstruct a sequence of events that occurred during the First World War in an effort to locate her fiancé, who turns out to be alive but suffering from amnesia. In *Alien Resurrection*, Ripley's memories, inexplicable in individual terms, since she is a newly formed clone, are described as "generational," a kind of collective memory that transcends the individual. This could be an allegory for the role of history in Jeunet's films. The eras to which we are taken back are those surrounding the World Wars, but, in the case of *Delicatessen*, there is an additional historical allusion, through the ubiquitous presence of television (suggestive of the late 1950s and early 1960s) and the use of Nouvelle Vague iconography, to the Algerian War (1954–62), which was as divisive as the Second World War to the French.

Although the ubiquity of television in *Delicatessen* points diegetically to the future (in relation to the film's setting), for viewers of the film it functions as a kind of "screen memory" that at once deflects from and hints at a repressed past. Jeunet's films make much use of screens-within-the-screen, often including archival film and television footage (beginning with *Pas de repos pour Billy Brakko* and *Foutaises* and culminating in *Delicatessen, Amélie,* and *Un Long dimanche de fiançailles*). This technique evokes what Alison Landsberg calls "prosthetic memory," or the blurring of the boundary between individual memory and mediatized representations of historical events. In Jeunet's films, this boundary is constantly blurred, increasingly so in the wake of the development of computer-based technologies such as CGI and digital technology, which Jeunet has used liberally since *La Cité des enfants perdus.* These technologies, which are a form of animation (involving the creation rather than the recording of an image), take Jeunet back full circle to the animated shorts made with Marc Caro, which often—and with an almost eerie appropriateness—highlight the theme of the eternal return.

Early Short Films: The Eternal Return

Many of the themes and motifs that characterize Jeunet's later work are evident in the early short films he made with Marc Caro. Animation and collage techniques are foregrounded, as the filmmakers experimented with archival stock and puppets (the latter having particular resonance in France, with its strong *Grand Guignol* tradition, similar to Punch and Judy, still alive and well in public spaces such as the Luxembourg Gardens in Paris). The films invoke generic conventions such as the horror film, the hard-boiled detective thriller, the war film, and the filmed essay, and all are marked by a strong evocation of childhood, whether in the fears and anxieties expressed in the earlier, more sinister films or the whimsy and nostalgia of the later *Billy Brakko* and *Foutaises*, which are ultimately undercut by a healthy dose of irony.

L'évasion (1978)

In this short, animated puppet film, a prisoner, incarcerated in the Prison de la Santé in Paris, lives in hope of escaping. At night, he wanders through the underground passageways, desperately trying to pry open doors and cut through the bars in search of a possible way out. In their first collaborative effort, Jeunet and Caro explore a theme that will haunt them over the course of their creative partnership: the horror of confined spaces from which escape is difficult or impossible (*Bunker de la derniere rafale, Delicatessen, La Cité des enfants perdus*). This twinned theme of confinement and escape figures prominently in Jeunet's subsequent work, notably *Alien Resurrection*, in which the crew of an alien-infested spaceship tries to escape from the monsters, and in *Un Long dimanche de fiançailles*, which shows soldiers desperate to escape from the trenches by any means possible.

Le Manège (1979)

This puppet animation, written and directed by Jeunet with marionettes designed and operated by Marc Caro, won the César (the French equivalent of an Oscar) for best short film in 1981. On a dark, rainy night, children ride a merry-go-round, where they compete to grab a brass ring; the children are then taken beneath the merry-go-round, where they are condemned to turn the crank that makes it go around. This film thematically prefigures *La Cité des enfants perdus* in its depiction of the exploitation of children, its atmospheric evocation of the German expressionist style, and its lugubrious fairground setting. The film places itself on the dark side of childhood innocence. The merry-go-round evokes the idea of an endless cycle, which will be revisited in the pair's next film, *Le Bunker de la dernière rafale* (as well as in the theme of resurrection in *Pas de repos pour Billy Brakko* and again in *Alien Resurrection*).

Le Bunker de la dernière rafale (1981)

The film director Jean-Jacques Zilbermann has described how, when he was managing the Escurial cinema in Paris before becoming a director, he agreed to show Jeunet and Caro's first short film, *Le Bunker de la dernière rafale*, as an accompaniment to the feature film *Eraserhead* (dir. David Lynch; 1977). The double bill stayed on the program for seven years, until eventually, Jeunet and Caro's film became the main draw, with audiences purchasing tickets specifically to see it rather than the Lynch film (Drubigny).

As its title suggests, this short film is set in a confined space, like much of the action in Jeunet's films. *Delicatessen* is set entirely in a single apartment building; *La Cité des enfants perdus* is set in the confines of an oil rig and submarine; and *Alien Resurrection* is set in two spaceships. Although *Amélie* goes farther afield in terms of location than its predecessors, its action remains largely confined to the Montmartre area of Paris. And in *Un Long dimanche de fiançailles*, although several locations and settings across France and Corsica are used, a significant portion of the action takes place in the trenches. A large portion of *Life of Pi* is set on a lifeboat floating in the sea. Of course, restricted spaces have the virtue of being inexpensive to film, but it is not necessarily the case that Jeunet's films have increased their number of locations as their budgets have risen: *Alien Resurrection* and *Life of Pi*, both American-financed, big-budget productions, are set largely in extremely confined spaces.

In *Le Bunker de la dernière rafale*, this claustrophobia serves the story well, providing motivation for the soldiers' paranoia. It also contributes to the uncanny atmosphere, inspired by German expressionist films such as *The Cabinet of Dr. Caligari* (dir. Robert Weine; 1920) and *Nosferatu* (dir. F. W. Murnau; 1922). The use of black-and-white film stock and starkly contrasting lighting with lots of shadows further reinforces these allusions, as do the First World War–era uniforms and the bald commander, who evokes the German general played by Erich von Stroheim in Jean Renoir's First World War epic *La Grande illusion* (1938). At the same time, these allusions to a specific period of history are destabilized by anachronistic references to other periods (in particular, the 1950s B-movie aesthetic evoked by the film's use of somewhat primitive graphics, the 1970s punk skinhead fashions, and the rare but striking flashes of color). The primary allusion, however, is to the Second World War, conjured up especially by the images of human experimentation (invoking Chris Marker's 1961 *La Jetée*). Military scientists store collections of surgical implements, body parts, and prosthetic limbs, anticipating the military-surgical connection in *Alien Resurrection* as well as the collection of anatomical artefacts shown in *Foutaises*. The wheelchair-bound commanding officer announces the fascination with physical infirmity that figures in nearly all of Jeunet's films, and the emphasis on prosthetic limbs establishes an enduring preoccupation with the technological replacement and extension of organic processes.

In the laboratory where human experiments are conducted, an anatomical chart of the male reproductive organs is displayed prominently. This literal display of masculinity (in its stark, biological form) reduces military activity to the testosterone-fueled antics of adolescent machismo (the soldiers' brutish behavior is underscored when they physically attack each other in a childish dispute). The anatomical chart also prefigures similar charts of the female reproductive system shown briefly in *Foutaises* and *Amélie*, though the latter images are associated with expressions of aversion, whereas the male anatomy is not. The drawing of the phallus in *Bunker* also anticipates the graffiti of the ejaculating phallus in *Foutaises*, which is used to undermine the idea of children's innocence. But whereas in the later film the image highlights the adult savvy of children (prefiguring the sophisticated children in *La Cité des enfants perdus*), in *Bunker* the drawing emphasizes the puerility of the soldiers.

Finally, the title evokes a recurring conceit in Jeunet's work. The word *dernière* (last) is undermined by an ending that does not offer closure but instead suggests that the gunfight, far from being the "last," will be repeated in an endless loop. This idea of a cyclical return goes

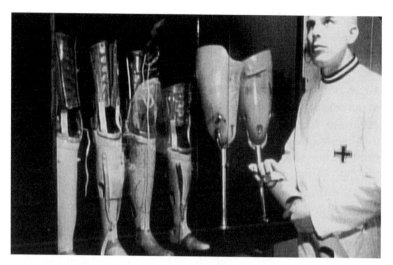

Figure 1. Prosthetic limbs in *Le Bunker de la dernière rafale.*

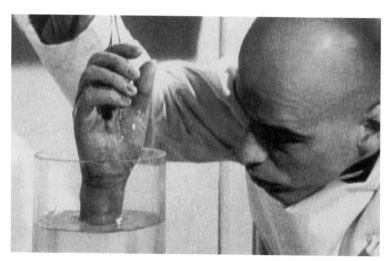

Figure 2. Lending a hand in *Le Bunker de la dernière rafale.*

hand in hand with the film's use of anachronism and prefigures the uncertain temporal settings of the later films.

Pas de repos pour Billy Brakko (1984)

Approximately four and a half minutes long, this film foreshadows some of the collage techniques that Jeunet would use in his next short film with Caro, *Foutaises*, and two decades later in *Amélie* and *Un Long dimanche de fiançailles*. Unlike *Bunker*, this short, narrated film speeds along at a breakneck pace, cramming in a wide range of images, sounds, and allusions to popular culture. Based on a comic strip created by Marc Caro, *Pas de linceuil pour Billy Brakko* (No shroud for Billy Brakko), and written, directed, and edited by Jeunet, the film is essentially an homage to the art of animation. The plot is somewhat convoluted and almost incidental to the riot of visual and aural detail. A man reads about his own death in the newspaper and then sees his own ashes at a crematorium. The voiceover notes: "In fact, what he'd really like is to bury himself in his inkpot like Coco the clown. He'd meet up with Betty Boop, who would sing 'Boopy doopy doopy doop! Boop boopy doo.' Only, this isn't a cartoon. It's a real film." In a pastiche of film noir, Brakko is tracked down by gangsters in 1930s-style cars and finally shot. The narrator intones, "He dies, and that's the end. . . . Or, if you prefer . . . ," and then tells of a committee consisting of several major cartoon characters, including Donald Duck and Felix the Cat, that decides to make an exception and allow Billy to "live in cartoon land, where the hero never dies." The narrator concludes, addressing the viewer directly: "It's your choice."

Encapsulated in this invitation to viewers to choose Billy's fate—and, by extension, the kind of film (tragedy or comedy) they want this to be— is an invocation of the fantastic, antinaturalist aesthetic that dominates most of Jeunet's films. This early film exhibits an *Amélie*-like preference for the idealized, limitless world of the imagination and for the "artificially arranged scenes" that have been associated with the fantastic since the era of Georges Méliès. It also displays a predilection for resurrection, which we will see again in *Alien Resurrection* and *Un Long dimanche de fiançailles*, when Manech is seemingly "brought back from the dead" in an unlikely twist of fate. The Soviet-inspired sequences in the film (including Julie, the "Eastern spy") anticipate the Eastern European flavor of *La Cité des enfants perdus*. The homage to the great masters of animation gestures toward the importance of animation techniques, including CGI, in Jeunet's later work.

Foutaises (1989)

This short film, which features Dominique Pinon and two other regulars from Jeunet's "band," Marie-Laure Dougnac (Julie in *Delicatessen*) and Chick Ortega (the postman in *Delicatessen*), won the César award for best short subject in 1991. Jeunet wrote the film with Bruno Delbonnel, who would become the director of photography on his later films. Though only eight minutes long, the film is a riot of ideas, gags, and vignettes, any two or three of which could have comprised an entire feature-length film.

Foutaises is composed entirely of the Dominique Pinon character (who is not named) announcing his personal likes and dislikes in a tongue-in-cheek reprisal of his memorable role as the small-time crook in *Diva* who is forever announcing the things he does not like. The opening credits are accompanied by shots of various cuts of meat in a butcher shop, a setting that features heavily in *Delicatessen*. The device of using visual puns to denote the various filmmaking roles being credited—such as, for example, a tray of eyeballs for lighting, pigs' ears for sound and music, cow brains for script writing, and a cleaver for cutting and editing—will also be used in *Delicatessen* (where the discarded contents of a garbage can perform the same function) and *Amélie* (where the games played by *Amélie* as a child mirror the production roles in the credits). In its use of the "likes and dislikes" conceit, the film presents a condensed prototype of *Amélie,* minus the guiding narrative thread (Jeunet has remarked in interviews that he collected disparate ideas for sequences in *Amélie* for several years before finding a plot with which to link them together).

The "likes and dislikes" conceit, which employs the technique of anaphora, or repetition of a phrase for rhetorical effect, invokes a literary exercise by the experimental French writer Georges Perec entitled "J'aime, je n'aime pas" (Perec 38–39). This allusion is bolstered by the statement, "I like biting off the ears of butter biscuits," which is identical to a line in Perec's novel *La Vie mode d'emploi* (Life: a user's manual; 1978) and underscores the presence of another work by Perec, *Je me souviens* (I remember; 1978), the book shown as the narrator states,

"I like finding sand between the pages of a book." *Je me souviens* is a catalog of seemingly random reminiscences, each beginning with the title phrase. The literary form of the catalog (employed in French literature as early as the litanies in Rabelais's *Gargantua* and *Pantagruel* in the sixteenth century) is self-consciously referred to in the film's use of images taken from the Manufrance catalog (a French equivalent of the old Sears Roebuck catalog).

The visual style of *Foutaises* resembles that of many of Jeunet's other films. The use of black and white recalls *Le Bunker de la dernière rafale* and hints at the restricted color palettes of Jeunet's later films. The Pinon character announces his preferences either directly to camera or in voiceover, with highly constructed studio sequences or inserts of stock footage and fast-paced, rhythmic editing. The combined effect of the rhythmic editing and montages of stock footage extends the collage aesthetic of *Billy Brakko* and prefigures sequences in *Amélie* and *Un Long dimanche de fiançailles*. The fast pacing reinforces the idea of a litany, almost overwhelming in its accumulation. This is the first explicit invocation of the idea of the collection, which figures prominently in Jeunet's later work (for example, the diver in *La Cité des enfants perdus* who collects and carefully labels discarded objects he finds in the sea; the box of childhood mementos in *Amélie*, as well as Nino's album and collections of photographs of drying cement and recordings of unusual laughs; and a similar box of mementos belonging to the condemned soldiers in *Un Long dimanche de fiançailles*). The idea of the collection culminates in the room full of botched clone prototypes in *Alien Resurrection*.

In *Foutaises*, a similar uncanny dread is invoked when the Pinon character expresses horror at the thought of his cousin's collection of anatomical curios: "Fingernail clippings, tufts of hair, facial hair fluff, appendix, and little bottles of tears." These body parts are kept in jars on a shelf, not unlike the cuts of meat and offal in the butcher shop, in reference to which the Pinon character utters the film's first line: "I don't like the things you see in the glass cases at the butcher shop. Yuck." The film thus opens on an expression of abjection, which figures strongly in *Alien Resurrection*. There is a similar sense of repulsion in *Foutaises* when the Pinon character informs us that, when "making love with a woman," he doesn't like thinking about "what's inside." An erotic image of a naked woman's torso is followed by an insert of an antique-style anatomical chart showing the female reproductive system. Screams of horror accompany the visuals and are still audible as the anatomical chart is replaced by drawings of men's hats from the antiquated Manufrance catalog, followed by a similarly styled illustration of a dog's muzzle. The items shown—the hats and the muzzle—are all designed to hold things in, to "put a lid on it," as though to compensate for a naked female body whose insides threaten to spill out. In a similar vein, one of the first "likes" that the narrator expresses is of pulling his socks up—another attempt to keep the internal contents of the body from spilling out. The horrific screams heard here echo those heard minutes earlier as the narrator describes his dislike of plucking his own nose hairs. The earlier screams appear to be the result of physical pain, but their exaggerated effect is connected with a horror of externalizing an internal fragment of the body—like the effect of the uncanny, which Freud, paraphrasing Friedrich Wilhelm Joseph von Schelling, described as "something which ought to have been kept concealed but which has nevertheless come to light" (Freud 394). This sexual squeamishness will surface again, with the aid of a similar anatomical chart, in the introduction to the repressed, hypochondriacal café clerk Georgette in *Amélie*, who, we are told, does not like the expression "the fruit of thy womb." And it will be literally turned inside-out in *Alien Resurrection*, with its abundance of slime and alien babies exploding out of abdomens. As the narrator in *Foutaises* screams in terror, we see stock footage of collapsing phallic structures, tongue-in-cheek allusions to the castration complex supposedly triggered by the sight of the female genitals.

The wish not to know "what's inside" is also an expression of romantic idealism, of a desire to focus on the glossy exterior instead of delving deep into the structure of things. When the Pinon character expresses his dislike of the butcher-shop display, it is not because he is a vegetarian (he announces his love of peeling ham off of wax paper and popping it into his mouth); it is because he does not want to know the gory details of the process by which the meat makes its way to the wax paper. But at the same time, this romantic idealism is undermined by the sequence immediately preceding the one about "women's insides." As a small child bounces a ball against a wall, the Pinon character expresses a fond appreciation of "the innocence of children"—but the camera moves closer to reveal a griffito of an ejaculating phallus on the wall, undermining the idea of a prelapsarian, presexual innocence of children. A similar undermining of innocence is to be found in the film's title (*foutaises* means "trifles" in the sense of silly, throwaway remarks, but the word stems from the verb *foutre,* which means "to screw"), whose vulgarity undercuts the tender nostalgia displayed within the film. The suggestion may be that viewers would do well to take any expressions of nostalgia (which we will see in all of Jeunet's films) with a grain of salt.

Cutting off the Past: Historical Trauma in *Delicatessen*

Throughout his career, Jeunet's work has been criticized for its perceived attention to style at the expense of content. Like the *cinéma du look* filmmakers, Jeunet has been taken to task for creating slick, glossy films with high production values and (so it is often claimed) little in the way of profundity. For example, Rita Kempley in the *Washington Post* declared that "[u]ltimately *Delicatessen* isn't about anything but Jeunet and Caro's filmmaking." However, Jeunet's first feature-length film is concerned with far more than its "look"—although many of its thematic concerns are conveyed *through* that look.

Delicatessen was Jeunet and Caro's breakthrough film. After years of making commercials, music videos, and short animated films, the pair were finally able to secure the backing to make their first full-length feature. They had already written the screenplay for *La Cité des enfants perdus,* but the elaborate special effects and enormous sets the film would require were deemed too costly and elaborate for a first film. When Jeunet and Caro made their pitch for *Delicatessen* to Claudie Ossard, who would go on to produce *La Cité des enfants perdus* and *Amélie,* they presented their ideas on a piece of butcher's paper. Jeunet recalls that "[i]t took a very, very long time to find the funding to make *Delicatessen.* I remember that we would call [Ossard] every morning, and we would say, 'So, how's it going? Are things looking good?' And it was because of this passion, this conviction, this tenacity, that she was herself motivated, and that made her persist" (Drubigny). When the film finally opened in 1991, it received glowing reviews in France and was nominated for ten César awards, winning four of them.

Jeunet has spoken often of the inspiration for *Delicatessen.* The idea came to him when he lived in an apartment above a butcher shop. Every morning, he was woken by a hacking sound; his girlfriend commented that the butcher must be chopping up the residents of the building one by one, and it would be their turn soon. *Delicatessen* tells the story of a butcher who supplements his meat supply with handymen who come to work in the building he owns, until his daughter falls in love with a former circus clown designated as her father's next victim. Although set in an indeterminate, postapocalyptic future, the film contains many unmistakable references to the Second World War. The costumes and hairstyles evoke the 1940s, as does the taxi in which (or pushing which) Louison arrives; the sepia tones of the color palette recall early experiments with color photography. The newspaper *Les Temps difficiles* (Hard times) is an explicit reference to the underground publications of the various branches of the Resistance movement. The broadcasting of coded messages on the wireless radio and even the presence of a (literally) underground movement are unmistakable allusions the war (see Hayes). The butcher—referred to simply as "Boucher"—evokes Klaus Barbie's macabre nickname, the "butcher of Lyon." The reference to Germany is spelled out in the film's title, a German word that stands out because it is a word for which there is a perfectly common French translation (*charcuterie*). Graeme Hayes points out that the foreignness of the word *delicatessen* serves to heighten the viewer's sense of disorientation in relation to the film's temporal and spatial setting (Hayes 200). The word is indeed disorienting, as it invokes not only German identity but also transnational identity, because it is a word that circulates widely outside its country of origin.

When Jeunet and Caro began filming *Delicatessen* in 1991, France was still reeling from the Klaus Barbie trial, which had taken place in 1987. What began as an apparently straightforward case against a known war criminal for crimes against humanity ended up with the French nation itself on trial for its complicity in the Holocaust. The Barbie trial shattered the long-standing silence that had surrounded the events of the war, opening up a Pandora's box of collective guilt and self-recrimination. *Delicatessen* was made at the height of the period that Henry Rousso has termed France's era of "obsession" with its collaborationist past (Rousso 155–94). But its production also came at a time when the French were beginning to acknowledge state-sanctioned atrocities committed during the Algerian War, and the film also evokes this other traumatic episode in French history.

The film's central image of cannibalism perfectly captures the stifling atmosphere of wartime privation in everyday life and the overwhelming preoccupation with ensuring an adequate supply of basic provisions. But the image also resonates with other meanings. In the French humanist tradition of *les belles lettres,* cannibalism evokes the classic essay by Montaigne, "Des Cannibales," that all French schoolchildren read at some point in their educational careers. Writing during the Wars of Religion in the late sixteenth century, Montaigne uses the image of cannibalism to challenge exoticist assumptions about peoples traditionally considered to be "savage" by exposing the potential for barbarity within so-called civilized society. Although absolutist in his condemnation of tyranny and cruelty, Montaigne endorsed a kind of cultural relativism based on historical context in which strict dichotomies (us versus them; good versus evil) were shown to be more fluid than they initially appeared. Jeunet seems to be making a similar point in *Delicatessen* concerning the opposition between the Germans (as perpetrators) and the French (as victims) during the Second World War, as well as the opposition between resistors and collaborators within France. Evil, Jeunet's film suggests, can be located within the French cultural memory rather than projected outward. Rousso explains why such internal battles are so difficult to overcome: "On the whole, the fratricidal conflicts of the Occupation were not a 'cold civil war' or a 'verbal civil war' but a civil war, period, on the scale of French history. And civil wars have always been the hardest to recover from, because, unlike war against a foreign power, the 'enemy' is still around after the battle" (Rousso 18). Cannibalism is thus an apt metaphor for a society turned on itself.

As Alain Finkielkraut has written, in postwar France "the collective consciousness was too busy transforming the unsavory reality of the Occupation into the myth of a populace united in glorious opposition against a common Enemy to pay attention to the specificity of genocide" (Finkielkraut 37). The willful "overlooking" of this specificity contributed, according to cultural critics such as Finkielkraut and Rousso, to a long-lasting cultural malaise. The erasure of traumatic events such as those associated with war triggers a psychopathological process known as incorporation, which Nicolas Abraham and Maria Torok describe thus: "[I]n order not to have to 'swallow' a loss, we fantasize swallowing (or having swallowed) that which has been lost, as if it were some kind of thing" (Abraham and Torok 126). The long silence surrounding France's complicity in the events of the war is figured in *Delicatessen* as a form of anthropophagy: "Failing to feed itself on words to be exchanged with others, the mouth absorbs in fantasy all or part of a person" (Abraham and Torok 128). As a vegetarian, Louison remains outside the cannibalistic economy; and he is, perhaps not coincidentally, the only character whose past is explicitly invoked (by means of photo albums, posters and photos on the wall of his room, and his televised circus performance, which accompanies the film's climactic rooftop struggle). Louison is also the only character who gives full expression to his grief: he mourns the loss of his show-business partner Livingstone, a chimpanzee eaten by the circus owners. Louison's successfully completed mourning stands in stark contrast to that of the Tapioca family, whose incipient attempt to acknowledge the death of the children's grandmother is cut short by the butcher, who shoos them out of his shop. This is why it is Louison who is able to break the circle of violence in the community: he is the only one who does not repeat the violence by denying or repressing it.

The motif of cannibalism thus serves as an allegory for France's inability to own up to its history. According to Naomi Greene, "erased from the ledger of history" were "the bitter civil warfare of the 1940s; the brutalities of the *Milice* [the French paramilitary force that fought against the Resistance movement]; the heroic and vital role played by the British; French anti-Semitic legislation and deportation of Jews; widespread enthusiasm for Pétain; [and] divisions within the Resistance" (Greene 70). The terms of the debate about the war are rehearsed in an exchange between Julie and Louison, while the butcher eavesdrops. When Julie asks Louison if he has forgiven the people responsible for killing and eating Livingstone, he replies, "We must always be able to forgive." She counters, "That depends. Sometimes it's impossible to forgive." Louison retorts, "You mustn't say that. No one is all bad. It's the circumstances that are bad." This exchange echoes polemics about the culpability of ordinary French people during the Collaborationist era and, more acutely, about people directly involved in the administration and execution of the atrocities of the war. For example, Jacques Vergès,

Klaus Barbie's defense lawyer, argued that Barbie's crimes were no different from those of the French state, which had sanctioned all manner of atrocities in the name of its colonial "civilizing mission." According to Alain Finkielkraut, Vergès "wanted, in a word, to show that there was neither angel nor demon, neither absolute villain nor saintly hero, and that the 'butcher of Lyon' was the sacrificial victim of our mythology, the scapegoat we required in order to pinpoint the abjection, and to exorcize the evil all around us by means of a reassuring manicheanism" (Finkielkraut 72). If we apply this line of argument to *Delicatessen*, the butcher is made the sacrificial victim of the collective to atone for its complicity in a corrupt system.

In *Delicatessen*, cannibalism is a practice in which most residents of the apartment building participate (with the notable exception of Louison, who announces his vegetarianism at the outset; the Troglodistes, a vegetarian underground resistance group; and Julie, the butcher's daughter, who expresses her strong disapproval of her father's practice). The anthropophagic residents come from all walks of life and seem to represent a cross-section of French society: the self-sufficient artisans and peasants; the brothers who make animal toys in their apartment; the man who subsists on snails and frogs in the attic; the working-class Tapioca family, reduced to recycling used condoms; the flirtatious Mademoiselle Plusse, who trades sexual favors with the butcher in exchange for choice cuts of meat; the comfortable petit-bourgeois butcher and his daughter; and the Interligators, the posh, upper-middle-class (possibly aristocratic) married couple. The sin is thus communal, and the unhealed wounds, figured in the motif of butchery, come back to haunt. Although the French would cut themselves off from their dark past, it insinuates itself obliquely, "bleeding" through to the present.

For all its sinister innuendo, we never actually see an act of butchery or cannibalism, and there is virtually no carnage in the film (with the exception of Julie's nightmare, in which Louison's throat is slit—but even this scene is relatively discreet). The horrific menace of the film's precredit opening sequence is never borne out, or at least not on screen: we see the butcher's cleaver rise and fall, and we know what (or who) is its target, but we are spared the gory details. The only violence we actually witness occurs at the end of the film, when the butcher is fatally wounded by his own hand. Otherwise, the mutilation that is constantly threatened is either performed off-screen (literally, "obscenely") or is endlessly deferred, like the death that repeatedly eludes the suicidal woman Aurore, despite the increasing lengths to which she goes in her efforts to kill herself. There are only two instances in which we see the aftermath of mutilation, and both of these are incidental: in one case, the result of an accident, we see the stump of Robert's leg that was cut off when he happened to get in the way of the butcher's murderous work; and in the other case, we catch a brief glimpse of a severed hand, which presumably once belonged to the butcher's latest victim, nestling discreetly among the litter in a garbage can during the opening credits—a reversal of the image of Robert Kube's stump, because it shows what has been taken rather than what remains. With its lingering shot of the contents of a trash container, the opening credit sequence immediately establishes an underlying motif of *refuse*, that which has been rejected. The severed hand appears so briefly that it is easy to miss. (This motif will appear again in *Amélie* in the figure of Lucien, the grocer's assistant with the withered arm, and more explicitly in *Un Long dimanche de fiançailles*, where we see soldiers blowing off their own hands.) The merging of mutilation with that which has been discarded creates an overdetermined image that points to repression on a number of levels: repression of the memory of physical violence; repression of the ideological and political divisions between collaborators and resistants; and repression of the fact of the repression itself. That the severed member has been discarded suggests a failure to recognize that repression has occurred, a denial of the severing of ties with the past—the mutilation or cutting off of the past is itself discarded, repressed, and unacknowledged.

The film opens with shots of bombed buildings reduced to rubble. The apocalypse has already occurred, and we are thrown into the period of *le deuil inachevé* (unfinished mourning) that Rousso describes as France's initial response to the war (figure 3). The inhabitants of the apartment building seem almost resigned to their deprivation, and there is no explicit mention of the human slaughter that is occurring under their roof. The *refoulement* (repression) that Rousso identifies as the second stage of France's struggle to come to terms with the war is expressed metaphorically in the image of the sodden attic filled with snails and frogs, the dark secrets of the unconscious. This space is a mirror image of the dank gutters inhabited by the Troglodistes. This claustrophobic, mildewy

Figure 3. The postapocalyptic
setting of *Delicatessen*.

space in which water collects and stagnates harbors symbols of French
national identity—snails and frogs, representing stereotypical French
cuisine, are elements of the culinary *patrimoine*. In the film's climax, the
water that has been building up is released, heralding the return of the
repressed, the phase that Rousso calls the "miroir brisé" (broken mirror)
in which illusions are shattered. A kind of purging has taken place, with
the cleansing of the collective conscience represented metaphorically
by the flood that engulfs the entire building (figure 4). This ending is
foreshadowed in the repeated emphasis on the role of pipes in the film,
from the opening precredit sequence, as the camera appears to move
up through a pipe, to the various scenes in which residents either listen
in on other conversations or talk to others through the pipes. Plumbing
functions as a key means of communication among the residents, and
the overflow of water at the end of the film represents a literal opening
up of the floodgates of traumatic memory and expression.

Of all the apartments in the building, only one is home to a traditional
nuclear family, comprising a mother, father, two young boys, and the
maternal grandmother. The Tapioca family provides a glimpse of the
domestic structure that is otherwise absent from the film. The building
is inhabited, at least initially, by single people (Julie, Louison, and the

Figure 4. The flood in *Delicatessen*.

attic-dwelling man who lives among the snails and frogs) and odd couples (the Interligators, who are childless and do not seem to speak much to each other; the toy-making Kube brothers, who clearly get on each other's nerves; and Mademoiselle Plusse and the butcher, whose relationship constitutes not a romantic rapport or even the spontaneous expression of desire so much as a sexual regime based on a power differential, in contrast to the relationship that gradually develops between Julie and Louison, which appears to be based on shared interests and mutual respect). Julie is motherless and feels only contempt for her father. By the end of the film, she has transferred any affection she may have had for her father to Louison. In the final scene, Julie and Louison form a happy family, as the pair are shown playing a duet on the sun-drenched rooftop of the apartment house a few feet away from the Tapioca boys, who appear to be playing the role of their surrogate children (figure 5).

There is a foreshadowing of this domestic scenario shortly after Louison's arrival, when he entertains the boys with soap bubbles after having confiscated a cigarette from one of them with a gentle reprimand. This is the moment at which Julie first encounters Louison, and she is clearly touched by his affectionate rapport with the children. Throughout the film, the butcher expresses his possessive attitude toward his daughter. When the postman comments that Julie "needs someone," the butcher

Figure 5. Domestic harmony in *Delicatessen*.

replies menacingly: "She has someone. Me." Ginette Vincendeau has
identified a commonplace of French cinema that extends back to the
postrevolutionary romantic era: "The influence of *Les Misérables* is clear,
and indeed its hero Jean Valjean, embodied by Harry Baur, Jean Gabin,
Lino Ventura et al., has haunted French cinema with his quest for his
'daughter' Cosette" (Vincendeau, "Fathers" 160). Vincendeau's allusion
to the family romance of the French Revolution is apt, as the butcher's
patriarchal role evokes not only Pétain but also Louis XVI (see Hunt).
In French historical iconography, blades are closely associated with the
execution of Louis XVI during the French Revolution, an association
reinforced by the name of the character Louison—"little Louis." Louison
bears some responsibility for the elimination of the patriarchal figure of
the butcher because it is his weapon, a boomerang-style knife, that kills
him. Only after Julie's father is safely out of the way can Louison and Julie
set up house together, and the collective expiation process can begin.

The butcher's patriarchal role is illustrated in the film's best-known
sequence, in which the rhythm of daily life is brought into step with the
sexual motions of the butcher and Mademoiselle Plusse. The residents'
movements, from a woman beating her rug to Louison painting the ceil-
ing, are synchronized to match those of the amorous couple. On a formal
level, the sequence functions as an atonal musical number. On a symbolic

level, the butcher is a Pétain figure: the sequence illustrates his "authority as controller of . . . the organisation of the entire community" (Hayes 203), evoking the Vichy regime's attempt to synchronize every aspect of public and private life to come in line with the policies exemplified in its motto, "Travail, Famille, Patrie" (Work, Family, Country). The comedic value of the sequence derives from what Henri Bergson describes as one of the laws governing the comic: "The attitudes, gestures, and movements of the human body are laughable in exact proportion as that body reminds us of a mere machine" (Bergson 79). It is the mechanical nature of the sexual encounter that makes it funny.

The mechanistic, functionalist effect that Bergson describes is also reflected in the proper names used in the film. Although the characters are not forthcoming in speaking about the horrors going on around them, their names articulate what they themselves cannot. Along with the butcher, referred to simply as "Boucher," the mailman and would-be suitor of the butcher's daughter is referred to as "Facteur" (mailman). These characters are defined through their jobs, as though they were merely cogs in the greater social machinery. In a visual version of this association between job title and personal identification, the opening credits show the names of the production crew inscribed on discarded objects in a garbage can that evoke their function: the screenplay credits are printed on the pages of a book; the director of photography is credited on a broken camera; the director of music on a shattered vinyl record; the sound supervisor on an old radio; costumes on a shirt label; and the editor on a torn strip of photo-booth photos that has been pieced back together. Although more particularizing than Boucher and Facteur, the names of other characters share with these anonymizing, descriptive names a Dickensian connotative function and are so obviously meant to furnish information about the characters that they border on the generic (and the comic). Perhaps most straightforwardly, the Tapioca family name signifies food, which has become an all-consuming preoccupation in an era of severe rationing. Then there are the Kube brothers, whose name, a homonym for "cube," suggests repetition (the tripling of numbers) and, as the slang term for a student forced to repeat the same year three times in a row, rote mindlessness, which is borne out in their endlessly repetitive toy making. Slightly more opaque is the last name of the woman who repeatedly attempts suicide and her husband, Interligator, which sounds much like *interrogateur* (interrogator) and thus evokes wartime intrigue, espionage, and torture. The name also suggests "ligature," a word with multiple meanings in both French and English. It can refer to binding or tying up—the opposite of multilation—in surgery (or sausage making) as well as in printing (a character combining two or more letters) and music (denoting a group of notes intended to be played or sung as a single phrase). Music unites Julie and Louison: their saw-and-cello duets, which occur at two key points in the film (the first instance confirming their mutual attraction and the second, in the final scene, signaling the solidity and durability of their union), signify their "harmonious" relationship. The metaphorical creation of social bonds or interaction is present in the idea of "tying up" suggested in the name Interligator, which adds a layer of irony to Aurore's macabre desire to cut herself off from the rest of the world. The Interligators do not appear to have much social interaction with their neighbors, nor do they appear to cohere as a couple, which compounds the irony of their name.

The antirealist aesthetic apparent in the proper names of the characters is also at work in the film's production design, which assumes a symbolic function and gives the film an ambiguous geographical and temporal setting. The setting is never named, and the little courtyard is completely isolated. When Louison first arrives in search of a job, the butcher explains that there are no neighbors in the area because, "Ici ou ailleurs, on est nulle part ici" (Whether here or there, this is nowhere). In the French DVD commentary, Jeunet refers to the location of the apartment building as "No Man's Land" (anticipating the First World War setting of *Un Long dimanche de fiançailles*). The apartment building in *Delicatessen*, like the bunker in *Bunker de la dernière rafale*, is self-contained. Its residents have little contact with the outside world. Even the radio "broadcasts" are confined to the building and its murky underground passages, and much of the communication between apartments is conducted via the building's internal plumbing system. Home is also the place of work; the Kube brothers' toy-manufacturing business is in their apartment, the butcher's shop is on the ground floor, and no one else appears to go out to work. Any strangers who penetrate the closed community do not come out, being literally incorporated, or ingested, by it. Even Louison, the outsider who manages to break the circle of violence, remains in the building at the end of the film. Referring to the poetic realist film by René Clair, Naomi Greene points out that, in *Delicatessen*, "[b]arricaded doors and claustrophobic terror-filled apartments have replaced the shared spaces—the streets, courtyards, and bistros—that figured so prominently in *Le million*. All that remains of the once vibrant city seen in that film are the dark and confining walls of the small apartment house" (Greene 184).

As unsettling as the film's lack of geographical specificity may be, its temporal ambiguity is even more disorienting and more heavily symbolic. As Mademoiselle Plusse remarks to Louison, "L'avenir, ça devient vite du passé par ici" (The future quickly becomes a thing of the past around here). Although ostensibly about the lack of hope among the residents of the building, Plusse's comment also reflects the film's blatant historical imprecision. This imprecision is achieved from the first scene after the opening credits, an establishing shot of the bombed-out ruins of a war-torn street. Unlike other European cities such as London and Dresden, the French capital was not bombed during the war. In this recasting of Paris as a bomb site, *Delicatessen* pays homage to the 1961 Chris Marker film *La Jetée*, whose indistinct futuristic setting was likewise strongly evocative of the Second World War, with German-speaking captors performing medical experiments on their French prisoner. (Jeunet would return to this image of a ruined Paris at the end of the alternative version of *Alien Resurrection*.) *Delicatessen's* images of Paris reduced to rubble recall two key post-Haussmann-era moments in the twentieth-century history of the city's transformation: the modernization of the city in the early 1960s, and Mitterrand's *grands travaux* of the 1980s and early 1990s, the time the film was made. *Delicatessen* evokes these eras of upheaval and transition, and this historical ambiguity results in disorientation.

According to Cathy Caruth, disorientation is a symptom of trauma, which enables "history to arise where immediate understanding may not" (Caruth 182). The ambiguous temporality of the film mirrors the way that the Barbie trial had bestowed upon the events of the war the status of a current event. In his essay on the trial, Alain Finkielkraut notes: "By placing us in the realm of the sentence and no longer simply in that of knowledge or commemoration, this judicial ceremony filled the abyss that separated us from the time of Barbie and his victims. By virtue of the fact that we awaited the verdict with them, we became their contemporaries. What took place more than forty years ago today found, in our presence, its epilogue" (Finkielkraut 12). Similarly, the film's uncertain placement in time prevents viewers from dismissing it as a "mere" period piece. Just when the specificity of the film's period details lulls you into thinking that you can pinpoint the time in which it is set, it eludes you, forcing you to conclude that if the film is not set in any particular era (or, perhaps more precisely, if it is set in *many* particular eras), the events it depicts could well happen now.

In *Delicatessen,* as in many of Jeunet's films, the seepage of the past into the present occurs in the use of anachronistic period details. These details bring out not only the period of the Second World War but also the 1930s, through its strong evocation of French films of that era, particularly those by René Clair and Jean Renoir. The cobblestoned, Second Empire courtyard set is evocative of Paris as seen in countless films of the 1930s, notably *Le Crime de Monsieur Lange* (dir. Jean Renoir; 1936). The dilapidated apartment building bears a strong resemblance to the building in which Jean Gabin holes up in *Le Jour se lève* (dir. Marcel Carné; 1939), as well as to the building that is at the center of René Clair's 1930 *Sous les toits de Paris.* The accordion music featured on the soundtrack also evokes this era.

Delicatessen invokes an even earlier entertainment form, already the site of nostalgic longing in films of the 1930s: the circus. From the opening title sequence, when the tinny notes of an organ grinder act as a cheerful counterpoint to the sinister tone of the initial scenes, the circus imbues the film with a nostalgic sense of childlike wonder and slapstick humor, with all the ambiguity that these entail. Louison is a circus clown by profession, and he is sometimes seen rehearsing his act or trying out new tricks, such as the rubber-cleaver-in-the-head routine that frightens Julie. His room is full of mementos of his time in the circus, from a poster to a photo album with pictures of himself in full clown gear with his chimpanzee sidekick. At the climax, the apartment residents watch a televised performance of Louison and Livingstone's circus act. Perhaps more than anything else, the exaggeratedly long and pointy clown shoes that Louison wears, after giving his civilian shoes to a taxi driver in lieu of payment, signal the circus as a central motif in the film. The circus or funfair is a recurring source of fascination to

Jeunet (and Caro), reappearing with unmistakable emphasis in *La Cité des enfants perdus* and more peripherally in *Amélie*.

The attention to earlier entertainment forms in *Delicatessen* is another way in which Jeunet evokes the cinema of the 1930s, which, according to Dudley Andrew and Steven Ungar, "obsessively" paid "tribute to traditional entertainment forms while promoting the cinema as their inevitable heir" (Andrew and Ungar 188–89). Andrew and Ungar note that "[t]he circus was old-fashioned in both its institutional structure and in its fare; it was bound to fall" after the advent of more mass-market-driven entertainment forms (223). The circus in Jeunet's films functions as a key site of nostalgia whose eclipse signaled a decline in communal values and social cohesion—in other words, a "loss of authenticity" that spawned a "nostalgia for intimate contact" (224). Yet the *fête foraine*, or traveling fair, which was the entertainment form out of which the modern circus developed, was also the primary venue for film exhibition in France before the advent of purpose-built cinemas around 1906. Thus, in their use of circus motifs, Jeunet's films evoke both the origins of the cinematic medium itself and the entertainment form that cinema replaced.

Naomi Greene notes that "Louison's former profession as a circus clown is also imbued with cherished memories of a bygone era. It evokes a time when entertainment was joyous and shared—when people went to the circus together instead of sitting, as they do in *Delicatessen*, in front of flickering blue television lights in isolated apartments" (Greene 183). It is significant that the climactic showdown between Louison and the butcher takes place on the roof and involves a TV antenna while the building's residents are happily watching a televised performance of the circus in which Louison worked. That the climax of *Delicatessen* occurs when the circus is being shown on television points to the profound tension (and complicity) in the film between traditional entertainment forms (the circus, hula dancing) and modern or postmodern forms (television, infomercials).

The frivolous TV programs in *Delicatessen* echo the lighthearted radio broadcasts that contrasted sharply with the dark mood of the period leading up to the Second World War. According to Andrew and Ungar, "The political tone set by so many newspapers through their editorials, satirical columns, and cartoons was seldom felt in radio broadcasts. As pastime or background, programs of songs were mainly escapist, catering to romantic fantasies, cheap exoticism, and mindless comedy at odds with the ever more somber mood of the decade" (Andrew and Ungar 184). That *Delicatessen* transfers the function of wartime diversion to television underscores its profound anachronism. Television functions anachronistically in the film not only on a technological level, in the use of remote controls, but also in the presence of television in the homes of such a wide range of social classes (figure 6). There is also the transhistorical implication that TV is lulling present-day viewers into the passive acceptance of morally dubious political regimes, such as fascism. The film presents a critique of the society of the spectacle: as long as the TV is broadcasting its treacly fare into their living rooms, the inhabitants of the apartment building, and viewers more generally, seem willing to accept, or at least not to criticize openly, the outrageous excesses of their political leaders. The apparent (and short-lived) unification of isolated individuals through the distraction that television provides is not unlike the film's synchronized lovemaking sequence, as the light entertainment holds the apartment residents in thrall, bending their thoughts, feelings, and actions to its own rhythms. Television is surely the ultimate form adopted by the culture industry that Max Horkheimer and Theodor Adorno described in *The Dialectic of Enlightenment*, which in 1944 anticipated the omnipotence of the new medium: "Films, radio, and magazines make up a system which is uniform as a whole and in every part. Even the aesthetic activities of political opposites are one in their enthusiastic obedience to the rhythm of the iron system" (Horkheimer and Adorno 120).

In *Delicatessen*, as in *La Cité des enfants perdus* and *Alien Resurrection*, the future looks very much like the past, but the presence of television in *Delicatessen* points forward again, to the 1950s and 1960s, when television first became widely available in French homes. The presence of televisions in most of the private apartments, regardless of class, is the most glaring and pointed anachronism in the film, and it is significant that television is the sign and site of such anachronism. The presence of television in the apartments blends prewar economic structures (in which home and work were not yet separated, as in the Kube brothers' toy-making business and the butcher's residence-cum-shop) with the postwar boom, which resulted in increasingly privatized,

Figure 6. Watching television in *Delicatessen*.

atomized lifestyles. Jeunet mixes a 1930s communal courtyard ethos (which was already nostalgic in the 1930s) with the atomized lives of postwar consumers.

Television in *Delicatessen* serves as a kind of wish fulfillment, performing the dreamwork of the deprived inhabitants of the apartment building by showing images of unobtainable food to starving residents of a war-torn city, as in *Amélie* it screens pictures of running, cycling, swimming, and dancing—activities that the Glass Man dares not do because of his infirmity. In both films, the television broadcasts images of the fantastical overcoming of limitations that enables disadvantaged people to participate fully and physically in the world (a world in which one-legged men can tap dance, newborn babies can swim, a horse can race in the Tour de France, and food appears magically on the dinner table). However, these wish fulfillments remain firmly in the realm of illusion, making the privations of real life seem all the more acute. Horkheimer and Adorno wrote of this phenomenon in the context of sexual titillation, but their remarks can easily apply to the endlessly deferred promise of enough to eat: "The culture industry does not sublimate; it represses. By repeatedly exposing the objects of desire, breasts in a clinging sweater or the naked torso of the athletic hero, it only stimulates the unsublimated forepleasures which habitual deprivation has long since reduced to a masochistic semblance. There is no erotic situation which, while insinuating and exciting, does not fail to indicate unmistakably that things can never go that far" (Horkheimer and Adorno 140). In *Delicatessen*, a tray groaning with cheeses revolves enticingly on a turntable as a jaunty tune plays. There is no plot, no action other than the exhibition of the food in all its glory. This is food as spectacle, something to be admired in and of itself: cinema of attractions. If the *cinéma du look* is about making us desire the image rather than about telling a story, then the revolving cheese trays, which represent the essence of an advertising aesthetic, constitute the *cinéma du look* in its purest form.

Sean Cubitt has written of the role of technology in *Delicatessen* in mediating—and strengthening—social bonds:

> The renewal of community, so common as a theme in the cinema of the French Popular Front during the 1930s, returns here in a new guise, one in which the mediating powers of technology are emphasised rather than their alienating effects as tools of an external, instrumental logic of capital. Revelling in the technological, the boys and the directors can revision community under the guise of retroengineered objects like the talismanic singing saw. Throughout the film, technologies like the painting machine formed from braces [suspenders] embody the emotional and social relations between characters. . . . [W]e have a humanistic view of the world carried out in the form of relations thoroughly mediated by technologies. (Cubitt 32)

Cubitt's perspicacious analysis is readily applicable to the "retroengineered" technologies he names, but it neglects the presence of television, the technology that plays the biggest role in mediating human relations. Television spectatorship in *Delicatessen* is atomized, a substitute for (and hindrance to) more sociable activities. Television is depicted as a largely solitary pleasure or else part of the furniture of everyday life, virtually ignored as people go about their business preparing dinner, arguing, or falling asleep. The only time television is shown to bring people together is when Louison invites Julie to watch his televised circus performance with him, but it is the communal form of the circus, rather than its televisual transmission, that enhances this sociability. More than anything else, television is the locus of inane promotional fare, prototypical infomercials whose function is to create a bond between viewers and products rather than among viewers.

One of these promotional programs takes the form of a commercial for Kraft processed cheese. Georges Interligator, watching the extended advertisement, expresses amazement at the innovative new product: "Aurore, you must come see this," he gushes. This sequence illustrates the contradictions of U.S. cultural hegemony, as bland, artificial cheese is peddled in France (renowned for its artisanally produced cheese) and seems almost as outlandish and fantastical as other aspects of the film that test the suspension of disbelief. Jeunet achieves a defamiliarization of the banal by elevating it to the level of the awe-inspiring. These infomercial prototypes take commodity fetishism to one of its logical extremes, dispensing with entertainment as a pretext for the display of products and presenting the products themselves as the main attraction. The disproportionate emphasis on food in these advertisements reinforces the connection made by Kristin Ross between the two rhetorics of consumption (digestive and economic), which link the large-scale transformation in French daily life that occurred in the postwar era to the imagery used to depict wartime privations: "In attempting to account for the frenetic turn to large-scale consumption in postwar French society, a popular biological metaphor prevails: the hungry, deprived France of the Occupation could now be sated; France was hungry, and now it could eat its fill; the starving organism, lacking all nourishment, could gorge on newfound abundance and prosperity. In this quasi-ubiquitous narrative of wartime deprivation, France appears as a natural organism, a ravenous animal. That its inhabitants should, in a very brief time, completely alter their way of life and embrace a set of alien habits and comportments determined by the acquisition of new, modern objects of consumption is seen to be a *natural, necessary* development" (Ross 71–72).

This transformation is hinted at in the scenes of the Kube brothers' home business, with its small-scale assembly line in which they make bleating farm-animal toys. The mechanization of the epitome of rural life suggests a comical gesture toward modernization and is a parodic invocation of Taylorization and of encroaching industrialization. France was still a predominantly agrarian society in the 1930s; the Kube brothers turn the barnyard itself into a machine.

The consumer objects shown in *Delicatessen* underscore the sense of anachronism in the film: not only televisions but Julie's large, American-style refrigerator and the postwar-model car in which (actually, pushing which) Louison arrives at the apartment building point to the postwar era of economic prosperity in France, which sits oddly with wartime privations. The excessive nature of this prosperity is highlighted when Julie accidentally breaks a vase and explains to Louison that she is not unduly concerned because, as her extreme nearsightedness leads her to break objects all the time, she has "doubles" of everything. The idea of identical consumer products points up the commodified nature of manufacturing, a connection reinforced by the fact that it is a skipping record—emblem of the age of mechanical reproduction and precursor to the scene in *La Cité des enfants perdus* where Krank dresses up as Santa and lip-synchs to a skipping record—that causes Julie to knock over the vase in the first place.

Ross posits a link between the rhetoric of consumerism and the "ideology of capitalist modernization, an ideology that presents the West as a model of completion, thus relegating the contingent and the accidental—the historical, in a word—to the exterior" (Ross 196). What gets pushed to the outside in the "developing-country" model is France's colonial legacy—a legacy that is invoked in *Delicatessen*'s allusions (through the ubiquitous presence of television, not widely available in France until the middle to late 1950s) to another historical trauma, the Algerian War (1954–62). This period was marked by events that the French are still having trouble coming to terms with, as the 2005 Michael Haneke film *Caché* (Hidden) makes clear. Naomi Greene explains that, "[f]rom the very first, [the Algerian War] . . . was shrouded in denial. Because de Gaulle would not admit that France was at 'war' with one of its own *départements,* the war was referred to by a variety of euphemisms; it was a 'peace-keeping operation,' a 'police action,' the 'Algerian drama'" (Greene 133). This euphemistic rendering of the war—the refusal to recognize it as a war—thus helped to obscure the brutality (the acts of torture and other atrocities) committed on its behalf.

The colonial era is invoked ironically in the name of Louison's partner in the "Cirque colonial," a chimpanzee called Livingstone, an unmistakable allusion to the African explorer David Livingstone (figure 7). France's complicity in the Second World War and its guilt over the

Figure 7. Poster for the Colonial Circus
in *Delicatessen*.

colonial era came together in the Barbie trial, in which Jacques Vergès, Barbie's defense lawyer, argued that it would be hypocritical to prosecute a foreigner for crimes against humanity when the French themselves were guilty of comparable crimes during the colonial era and the painful process of decolonization. With the presence of lawyers from former European colonial possessions (Algeria, Vietnam, and the Congo) on Barbie's defense team, the link between these two chapters of France's history was reinforced in the minds of the French public. Moreover, the *décalage* (time lag) suggested by the anachronistic presence of television in *Delicatessen* and its evocation of a displaced historical trauma strangely echo the decision to defer the televised broadcast of the Barbie trial. After much debate, it was decided that the trial could be filmed but that it could only be broadcast several years later (Finkielkraut 117). In fact, the trial was not televised until 2001, fourteen years after the guilty verdict was rendered (similarly, the trial of Paul Touvier, the French *milice* leader who ordered the execution of seven Jewish prisoners, took place in 1994 but was not broadcast until 2002). This temporal displacement of the televised trials echoes the anachronistic function of television in *Delicatessen* and the displacement of historical events in the public consciousness that are deemed too traumatic to be assimilated at the time of their occurrence.

Not long after the release of *Delicatessen,* Kristin Ross wrote of the repercussions of France's inability to come to terms with its colonial legacy and the central role that this plays in shaping the contemporary social and political landscape: "France's denial of the ways in which it was and is formed by colonialism, its insistence on separating itself off from what it views as an extraneous period irrelevant to its true national heritage, forms the basis of the neoracist consensus of today: the logic of segregation and expulsion that governs questions of immigration and attitudes toward immigrants in France" (Ross 196). This diachronic separation (the relegation of France's colonial past to a footnote outside of the official narrative of French national history) thus led to a synchronic separation (the physical and social segregation of immigrants on the margins of the city, and society, in the *banlieues*). Paul Gilroy has written compellingly of how colonialism paved the way for the Holocaust, arguing that "colonial societies and conflicts provided the context in which concentration camps emerged as a novel form of political administration, population management, warfare, and coerced labor" (Gilroy 60). *Delicatessen* similarly suggests that the forms of traumatic memory and repression that structured France's collective memory of the Second World War functioned in a similar way with regard to the violent era of decolonization. Like the Vichy Syndrome of which Rousso wrote so compellingly, France began showing signs of an incipient "Algeria Syndrome"—a breaking of the relative silence surrounding the fraught period of decolonization—around the time *Delicatessen* was made. It was only in 1992, for example, that the French Ministry of Defense granted public access to its archives on the Algerian War (see Donadey 230 n.12). Anne Donadey has argued that the attention directed toward the Second World War in the last thirty years of the twentieth century "may have been facilitated by the desire to cover up the double loss caused by the Algerian trauma: the loss of innocence (which had been regained by the erasure of memories of Vichy and the collaboration) due to the Nazi-like methods employed by the French military in the Algerian conflict and the loss of land that signified the end of France's status as an imperial power and thus signalled a crisis in French identity" (Donadey 218).

In his commentary on the 2001 French DVD of *Delicatessen,* Jeunet begins by saying that he must reach back in his memory to access this film he made ten years earlier. It is fitting that this film should prompt such an explicit invocation of memory and its difficult retrieval. It is fitting, too, that the film ends with an image of a saw (the musical saw that Louison plays in a duet with Julie on the roof). The saw reminds us of the mutilation and trauma of the past but, in this case, inflected with a different tonality, even a sweetness. It is also a symbol of the harmonious future that awaits Julie and Louison. The saw signifies on two levels—as an instrument of severing and thus a symbol of the will to forget past horrors, it also provides, paradoxically, a link to the past. It reminds us of past wounds as well as the repression of these wounds: the past may be violent, but refusing to remember it, the film suggests, is also an act of violence (figure 8).

"It's Hard to Be Original": *La Cité des enfants perdus*

Whereas *Delicatessen* centers on mutilation (both literally and meta-phorically as the severing of the past), Jeunet's second feature-length collaboration with Marc Caro, *La Cité des enfants perdus,* emphasizes the prostheses that serve as extensions of organic processes, attempting to compensate for what has been lost. This prosthetic vision encompasses the realms of artistic and human reproduction, both of which are rooted in a meditation on origins and authenticity. This film, more than any

Figure 8. Louison clowning around
in *Delicatessen.*

other by Jeunet (with or without Caro), displays its kinship with the films of Georges Méliès, the master of "artificially arranged scenes" (Frazer), in its appropriation of fairy-tale, fantasy, and science-fiction genres, its pioneering use of digitally produced special effects, its dark humor, and its appeal to the themes and concerns of childhood.

La Cité des enfants perdus has grown considerably in critical stature and cult status since its initial release in 1995. Jean-Jacques Zilbermann, the director of *Les Fautes d'Orthographe* (Bad spelling; 2004) and *L'Homme est une femme comme les autres* (A man is a woman; 1998), has commented: "People didn't like Kubrick's films when they first came out, but then they began to like them later. When I saw *La Cité des enfants perdus* the first time, I didn't like it at all. But then, when I saw it a second time (I was a projectionist, and I was screening it), I started to like it, and when I saw it for the third time, I fell in love with it" (Drubigny). When the film opened the 1995 Cannes Film Festival, however, it was given a distinctly frosty reception. Audiences had trouble following the plot, and although critics praised the film's technical innovation (with 144 digitally created shots, totaling seventeen minutes of screen time, it was the most highly digitalized French film of its time), many felt that the lavish visual effects came at the expense of narrative coherence.

It is true that not all the plot elements are straightforward. The story concerns a group of clones who live together on what appears to be an offshore oil rig near an unnamed, desolate harbor town. They are all the creations of a lone, amnesiac inventor who lives in a submarine and spends his days trawling the ocean floor in a diving suit collecting objects that have been lost or thrown into the sea. The inventor's clones all suffer from some form of mutation, having been cursed, according to the film's fairy-tale logic, by a "wicked genetic fairy." The self-proclaimed leader of the clone community, Krank, is himself a scientist and inventor (and thus a cross between Frankenstein and his monster) who, being unable to dream, devises elaborate machines with which to "steal" the dreams of children who have been kidnapped by a religious cult. In exchange for the children, Krank swaps camera lenses that the cult members wear on their faces after gouging out their own eyes at the behest of their maniacal leader. The protector of one of the children, a circus strongman named One, embarks on a quest to save the child he refers to as his "little brother." Along the way, One befriends one of the other kidnapped children, a precocious nine-year-old pickpocket named Miette who develops a crush on him.

This synopsis is greatly simplified and leaves out many colorful characters and plot elements; it is no wonder that audiences had trouble following the storyline. The film's accessibility was not helped by the fact that, like *Delicatessen*, *La Cité des enfants perdus* has an imprecise temporal and geographical setting: it takes place in an undisclosed location seemingly isolated from the rest of the world (figure 9). The film's harbor setting, combined with references to the Cyclops cult, inevitably invokes Polyphemus, the Cyclops blinded by Odysseus in *The Odyssey*. Polyphemus was the son of Poseidon, the god of the sea, which reinforces the film's use of marine imagery, to which Jeunet returns in *Un Long dimanche de fiançailles* in the scenes set in Brittany.

A vague international ambience further adds to the film's geographical ambiguity: one of the protagonists, who has an English name (One), is played by an American actor with a Russian accent; the film's villain has a German name (Krank); there are Greek letters (which playfully spell "Méliès") on one of the ships docked in the port; and Eastern European music is played in the local café. The film opens on a dark, Felliniesque carnival setting in which people perform in freak shows,

Figure 9. The port in *La Cité des enfants perdus*.

barkers hawk their wares, beggars work the crowds, and a strongman bursts out of his chains. Like *Delicatessen,* the film is set in an unspecified, dystopian future that looks a lot like the past: in this Jules Verne–inspired diegetic universe, human cloning is taken for granted, and machines exist to transfer dreams from one person to another; yet the Jean-Paul Gaultier–designed costumes and the sets evoke the period following the First World War. There are numerous nods to poetic realism, including the prevalence of wet, cobblestoned streets and the murky harbor setting; the 1930s-era costumes worn by the street-urchin children; and the "Jean Gabin moment" of One, who suddenly lashes out brutally at Miette (recalling Gabin's character in classic poetic realist films such as *La Bête humaine* and *Gueule d'amour*). The film's ambience also pays homage to German expressionism: as in Fritz Lang's *M* (1931), children disappear, kidnapped by a mysterious gang; and a carnivalesque, *Caligari*-like atmosphere pervades the film, which is presided over by a mad scientist. The production design, created by Marc Caro with sets by Jean Rabasse, conveys an atmosphere of antique science fiction.

In *La Cité des enfants perdus,* memory is given a physical presence in much the same way that dreams are represented as something that can be distilled and transferred in vaporous form from one body to another. The body functions as the site of memorial inscription, a kind of living monument (One's tattoo proclaiming his love for Miette, or the map inscribed on the Chinese man's head in the tattoo parlor). This writing on the body is extended to the visual style of the film itself, on whose surface the past is engraved through its production design, sets, costumes, lighting, and color palette. The elaborate sets in this film would be of the kind that Charles Affron and Mirella Affron describe as "artificial" in their articulation of the five levels of design intensity that characterize the majority of fiction films. *La Cité des enfants perdus* embodies a high degree of design intensity, which privileges the role of décor "beyond that of simply supporting the narrative" (Affron and Affron 36). Artificial sets have their origins in the work of Georges Méliès and serve an expressionistic function, "mediat[ing] the narrative relationships between the material and the emotional; they objectify a nexus between exterior and interior, between the physical and the psychological universe" (114–15).

This film, even more than *Delicatessen*, presents the past nostalgically, largely through the band of scrappy, photogenic children whose escapades recall those of the Katzenjammer Kids or the Little Rascals. The loving presentation of the harbor town reinforces this nostalgic vision. However, the evocation of the past in *Cité*, as in *Delicatessen* and *Un Long dimanche de fiançailles*, is not purely nostalgic. It is ambivalent and deeply fraught, evoking both the charm and the darkness of German expressionist cinema. Anton Kaes has argued that films made following the First World War reflected a sense of paranoia that stemmed from the enemy's invisible and all-pervasive presence in wartime trenches. Invoking Ernst Jünger's theory of "total mobilization," Kaes contends that the war mentality pervaded civilian life to the extent that enemies— in the form of criminals—were thought to be lurking in the shadows of the city streets (Kaes). The residents of the harbor town in *La Cité des enfants perdus* live in a state of constant terror that their children will be kidnapped, and the walls are plastered with posters of the missing youngsters. This is an era in which circuses come to town and strong men protect children, but the circuses conceal marauding kidnappers, and the strong men sometimes assault the children they are supposed to be protecting. In this film, dreams of Christmas treats and visits from Santa soon turn to nightmares. Childhood itself, which the film romanticizes on one level, is not without its difficulties; Miette and her friends have been abandoned to their own devices, made to roam the streets committing petty crimes. They are a lost generation.

The characters who populate the film are all "lost children" in different ways. Some are literally lost, like the children who have been kidnapped by the Cyclops cult, whose members are themselves "lost"— troubled individuals who eagerly look to their charlatan leader for a chance at salvation. The characters on the rig are the biotechnological creations of an amnesiac inventor holed up in a submarine and thus lost children in the sense that they are cut off from their biological history: there is Krank, the mad scientist who is incapable of dreaming; his "wife" Marthe, a dwarf; the six identical clones (all played by Dominique Pinon), who do his bidding (figure 10); and a brain called Irvin floating in a fish tank with a camera for eye(s) and gramophone trumpets for ears. *La Cité des enfants perdus* takes the circus imagery in *Delicatessen* to its freakish limits. Despite their quirks, the colorful characters that people the film could have come straight from central casting of the *cinéma du look*. Sue Harris has written that "[t]here is frequently a sense that the world of the *cinéma du look* constitutes a freak show, in which hastily drawn caricatures . . . have come to life. Indeed, character construction is inherently simplistic, closer to that of cartoons and fairy tales than to that of modern cinematic representation" (Harris, "Cinéma" 222). This "freak-show" atmosphere is apparent in the Octopus sisters (La Pieuvre), conjoined twins who share everything: when one inhales cigarette smoke, the other exhales it; when one samples a dish they are cooking, the other smacks her lips; when one has an itch, the other scratches her arm.

The proliferation of physical abnormalities, the result of genetic manipulation gone wrong, is also evoked in the name Krank ("illness" in German). The suggestion is that Krank's failure to dream is an illness, and that there is a strong link between this illness and his hyperrationality. Krank is a brilliant scientist, but his superior powers of reasoning have somehow perverted his poetic side, indeed, his humanity (he complains that he has no soul), as, by implication, excessive genetic manipulation and scientific meddling in the name of bodily perfection have produced genetically abnormal bodies. In *La Cité des enfants perdus*, the body is either absent (the disembodied brain), deformed (the conjoined twins),

Figure 10. Clones in *La Cité des enfants perdus*.

exaggerated (the circus strongman), equipped with prosthetic sensory organs (the Cyclops cult members who sport camera lenses for eyes and microphones for ears), or nonorganically produced (the clones). Rosi Braidotti has identified such freak-show aesthetics as the product of the "posthuman" era: "The fascination for the monstrous, the freaky body-double, is directly proportional to the suppression of images of both ugliness and disease in contemporary post-industrial culture. It is as if what we are chasing out the front door—the spectacles of the poor, fat, homeless, homosexual, black, dying, ageing, decaying, leaky body—were actually creeping in through the back window. The monstrous marks the 'return of the repressed' of techno-culture and as such is instrinsic to it" (Braidotti 200).

The "deformed" bodies with an exaggerated physical presence in *La Cité des enfants perdus* are thus the repressed side of dreams of biotechnological perfection. They represent at once the dangers of biotechnology (an increased risk of mutation) and that which biotechnology tries to eradicate (bodily imperfection). The conjoined women are the flipside of the identical clones because they have to share a body, as though there were not enough bodies to go around, whereas the clones represent an excess of bodies, what would be referred to as "meat by-products" in *Alien Resurrection*. The logical extension of the technological dream of disembodiment is Irvin, the bodiless brain (figure 11). Irvin perfectly illustrates the fact that, as Scott Bukatman notes, "[t]he body has long been the repressed content of science fiction, as the genre obsessively substitutes the rational for the corporeal, and the technological for the organic" (Bukatman 19). Irvin's prosthetic sensory organs (gramophone, camera lens, etc.) represent a substitution of technology for the organic body. The irony is that Irvin, though lacking in corporeality, is the film's moral conscience or "heart." Irvin plays the role of a Greek chorus: he may only have access to what the leader of the Cyclops cult calls "the world of appearances," but he seems to cut through to the essence of things.

Like most science-fiction films, *La Cité des enfants perdus* invites viewers to ponder what it means to be human. When Marthe asks the identical clones, "Are you or are you not men?" they answer literally, "No, we're not." Her question refers to their level of maturity (as in, "Are you man enough?"), but their answer refers to their status as the product of technology. Like Pinocchio, these clones long to be human.

Figure 11. Irvin the disembodied brain in
La Cité des enfants perdus.

When Irvin dupes one of the identical clones into thinking that he's "the original," he can barely contain his joy. In a world of copies, originality is a scarce commodity, and the singular is prized above all else—hence the name of the film's hero, One, whose name suggests that he is the antidote to the clones and doubles who people the film. One's humanity—his good-guy nobility, his great capacity for disinterested affection, his paternal instinct—is juxtaposed with the monstrosity of those who are not "one" but multiple. According to René Girard, "'[T]he double and the monster are one and the same being'" to the extent that "'there is no double who does not yield a monstrous aspect upon close scrutiny'" (qtd. in Telotte 155).

The horrific nature of this monstrosity is displayed in the film's opening title sequence, which begins with what appears to be a childhood dream come true: Santa Claus emerging from a fireplace to greet a small child who awaits him eagerly. The dream, however, soon turns into a nightmare, as one Santa after another emerges from the chimney (figure 12). The treacly music turns ominous, and the child's smile dissolves into hysterical tears. The nightmare is that there are several Santas where there should only be one. If the Santas had been elves or reindeer, or anything not assigned the status of the singular, the dream would not

Figure 12. Multiple Santas in *La Cité*
des enfants perdus.

have descended into horror. The dream of Santa Claus is predicated on
his aura of uniqueness: the moment the children realize that there can
be lots of Santas, each as real (or unreal) as the next, is the moment they
realize that Santa can be anyone and is no one. As this scene forcefully
demonstrates, if one Santa is good, several are uncanny.

Building upon the work of Otto Rank, Sigmund Freud speculated
about the phylogenetic origins of doubles (or multiples): "[T]he 'double'
was originally an insurance against destruction to the ego, an 'energetic
denial of the power of death,' as Rank says; and probably the 'immortal'
soul was the first 'double' of the body. This invention of doubling as a
preservation against extinction has its counterpart in the language of
dreams, which is fond of representing castration by a doubling or multiplication of a genital symbol; the same desire spurred on the ancient
Egyptians to the art of making images of the dead in some lasting material" (Freud 387). For Freud, however, the reassuring aspect of multiplicity was eventually transformed into its opposite, on a phylogenetic
level (in the development of civilization) and an ontogenetic level (the
maturation of the individual subject): "From having been an assurance
of immortality, [the double] becomes the ghastly harbinger of death"
(Freud 387).

Freud's interpretation of doubles or multiples as a residual expression of the desire for "preservation against extinction" enables us to interpret the multiple Santas as overcompensation for the loss of childhood "innocence" in the normal process of maturation (the small child in the scene appears already to have left behind the primary narcissism stage, because he finds the multiplication of Santas instantly horrifying). *La Cité des enfants perdus* privileges traits that it implicitly links to childhood: a sense of wonder and the capacity to dream. It is the capacity to dream that Krank, all but paralyzed by his hyperrationality, hopes to tap into by kidnapping children. Like Charlie Chaplin roller skating in the department store or messing around on the assembly line in *Modern Times,* the children manage to throw a spanner in the works at every turn, disrupting Krank's cold, instrumental reason: in this, their "innocence" appears to win out. Yet many of the children shown in the film are world-weary and, having been left to fend for themselves, behave in ways that suggest they have acquired a maturity beyond their years. They have exchanges that evoke encounters between adults in classic love triangles, as when the little boy who clearly has a crush on Miette confronts her about her romantic interest in One. Similarly, when One points out to Miette that she is too young to be considered a suitable romantic partner for him, she protests that she is "not that young." Correspondingly, One is depicted as being very childlike. Miette claims that he is "not that old," and his halting, heavily accented French and seeming imperviousness to efforts to seduce him reinforce his childlike simplicity and gentleness. One seems to embody a stereotypical, almost caricatural, masculine physical ideal, bursting out of his figure-hugging, Jean-Paul Gaultier sailor suits. He is a gentle giant, at once suggestively flirtatious and explicitly off-limits as a romantic partner for Miette: he tenderly massages her feet, but when she asks what he will be looking for in a wife, he explains that he will have to look for some shoes "in One's size."

Perhaps above all, the film's deployment of Oedipal themes most forcefully places emphasis on childhood and its difficult transitions. The central relationship between One and Miette emblematizes these themes. One gets "Miette pour la vie" (Miette forever) in a lovers' heart tattooed on his arm. When One and Miette are lying together under a blanket, he calls her his "petite soeur" (little sister) but then nuzzles her shoulder in a sexually ambiguous way. When she asks him what he is doing, he replies, "Radiateur." In an earlier scene, the femme fatale in the bar attempting to seduce One calls him a "Radiateur," a new word he practices saying repeatedly, with all its sexual innuendo (the woman implies that he is sexually charged, a dynamo). Thus, when One uses this word with Miette, it cannot be dissociated from its earlier, sexualized context. On the French DVD commentary, Jeunet mentions that when Angelo Badalamenti, who composed the music for the scene, first watched this exchange between Miette and One, he was concerned about the potential sexual innuendo but was "reassured" that the relationship was platonic when he saw the end of the scene. Jeunet dismisses this concern as anxious pandering to political correctness, but the scene, and the relationship between One and Miette more generally, is certainly sexually ambiguous.

This ambiguity is all the more disturbing in the context of the other exploitative parental substitutes that people the film. The Octopus twins are presented as quasi-maternal figures, complaining, as parents often do, about the lack of gratitude from the children they feel they have protected. But their resentment (expressed in the adage "Raise crows and they'll peck out your eyes") lacks justification, as the Octopus sisters only exploit the children in their charge. It is hinted that, as children, the twins were likewise exploited by a parental figure, the opium-addled flea-circus impresario Marcello, played by Jean-Claude Dreyfus (the butcher in *Delicatessen*), and the suggestion is that they are continuing a cycle. The principal children's names reflect their objectification. "Denrée" suggests a foodstuff, and he is shown to have an insatiable appetite, gnawing on food and, in one case, when he gnaws on a candle, inedible material, throughout the film. In the film's closing shot, as One, Miette, and company flee the burning rig in their boat, Denrée takes a bite out of a sausage and burps. This gesture might be a playful allusion to *Delicatessen,* but it also serves as a reminder of Denrée's tender age. Similarly, "Miette" means "crumb," a tiny bit of a larger portion of food. Miette would like to be part of a whole, a family. She appears self-sufficient in both practical and emotional terms in the first part of the film, but her vulnerability is gradually drawn out by One (a common occurrence—with overtones of *The Taming of the Shrew*—in films where a woman is progressively "tamed" by a man as she becomes emotionally involved with him).

Miette's complicated relationship with One evokes the overdetermined figure of Oedipus that lurks behind (or, at least, limps through) the film. Oedipus means "broken foot" in Greek, and Oedipus is the patron saint of the many infirmities in the film. The most frequently occurring physical impairment in *La Cité des enfants perdus* is blindness, which has explicit associations with the Sophoclean story of Oedipus, who, upon discovering that he has unwittingly killed his father and married his mother, gouges out his eyes. This scenario is played out on several occasions in the film. In a flashback, we see Krank attacking the inventor, or father-figure, who created him and who, in the ensuing struggle, bloodies Krank's eye. This scene is a culmination of several allusions to blindness in the film. The opening fairground scene contains a visual joke in which one blind man leads another. The men, we soon learn, are members of the notorious Cyclops cult, who snatch children and bustle them into a truck with a giant eye logo painted on it and who, after blinding themselves, wear video cameras strapped to their faces to form a "third eye" (figure 13). On more than one occasion, these cameras are ripped off, not only recalling the Octopus sisters' lament about eye-pecking crows but also mirroring the Oedipal eye-gouging and evoking the Sandman who plucks out children's eyes in E. T. A. Hoffmann's story of the same name, analyzed by Freud in his essay on the uncanny (and invoked by Krank in an unsuccessful effort to inspire sweet dreams that he can steal from a child). These images are reinforced by the recurring visual motif of the lighthouse, whose lone light blinks in the darkness. At a climactic moment, when One turns on Miette and a tear she sheds sets off a chain reaction of events that culminate in the death of the Octopus sisters, the light is extinguished. The film ends with an iris shot, a circle shrinking around Denrée as he takes a bite out of a sausage, a tongue-in-cheek (if somewhat far-fetched) suggestion of the association between blindness and castration.

Oedipus is a lost child, abandoned in the wilderness, separated from his biological parents, and then reunited with them in terrible ways. His tragedy is that he does not recognize his own flesh and blood, does not see what is familiar (or familial) in the two individuals he has murdered and married, respectively. Oedipus' story is also the story of the return of the repressed, the encounter with something whose suddenly remembered familiarity is deeply unsettling. His failure to

Figure 13. Cyclops cult members in
La Cité des enfants perdus.

see his own history in the two people he presumes not to know makes
him unable to respect the succession of generations. By marrying his
mother, he collapses the filiation, the very notion of generation, in
which the incest taboo is grounded. Like the multilayered temporali-
ties of Jeunet's films, in which history is flattened out into a film set,
diachrony is made synchronous in the story of Oedipus. This collapse
of generations is evoked in a scene in which Miette's dream comingles
with Krank's, resulting in an eerie, hybrid *danse macabre*. As Miette and
Krank start dancing somewhat violently in slow motion, Miette grows
into a young woman, then a more mature woman, then an old woman,
while Krank shrinks in stature and in age until he is a little boy. In a
structurally similar, if affectively different, collapse of generations, One
refers to Denrée repeatedly as his "petit frère" (little brother), but he
fulfils a paternal function toward the abandoned child, protecting him
and raising him as his own. One and Miette are (sometimes alternately,
sometimes simultaneously) father and daughter, siblings, and potential romantic partners. In the film's final scene, in which One, Miette,
and the other children escape on a boat as the rig goes up in flames
(anticipating Jeunet's latest film, *The Life of Pi*), One and Miette are

in a sense "riding off into the sunset," the nominal parents of the clan of children escaping with them (figure 14).

Family ties are extremely malleable in *La Cité des enfants perdus*. Early in the film, Krank and the identical clones are referred to as "frères" (brothers), all the creation of the same inventor, but Krank plays the role of patriarch, ordering the clones around and keeping them at his beck and call, fearful of his wrath. Similarly, the identical clones call Marthe, the dwarf, "Maman," and they call Irvin "Oncle," even though, by the same logic that makes Krank their "brother," Marthe and Irvin would also be their siblings. (There is a similar confusion in *Alien Resurrection* in the relationship between Ripley and the alien with whom she shares an extended, slimy embrace and who can be her child, grandchild, and/or lover.) The conjoined Octopus sisters are at once perverse (because exploitative) maternal figures to the kidnapped children, whom they train to be petty thieves for their own financial gain, and daughter figures to the flea-circus owner, who, it is suggested, similarly betrayed their trust by exploiting them as young women working in his circus.

Regardless of whether they are mothers, brothers, or lovers, all the clones and products of biotechnological reproduction in the film are "lost children," cut off from their progenitor. Meanwhile, the inventor

Figure 14. Escaping in the boat in
La Cité des enfants perdus.

of the clones is cut off from his own past through the loss of his memory, a loss that coincides with the time he spends underwater, in a metaphorical allusion to repression not unlike the underground passageways in *Delicatessen*. The inventor collects objects that people have lost or thrown into the sea and carefully dates and labels them (prefiguring Nino in *Amélie*, who collects discarded photographs from automated photo booths and arranges them in an album). The inventor in *Cité* calls himself a "grand chercheur," which literally means "a great searcher," as in treasure hunter or collector but also (and primarily) researcher. He maintains an archive of these curios in his submarine to compensate for his lost memory, like an archaeologist or historian who must make do with artifacts in the absence of direct access to the past. This compensatory function of the inventor's collection evokes the role of history, according to Pierre Nora, who, in his introduction to *Realms of Memory*, distinguishes between "true" memory and "artificial" history: "Memory is life, borne by living societies founded in its name. . . . History, on the other hand, is the reconstruction, always problematic and incomplete, of what is no longer" (Nora 8). History is thereby aligned with the origins of the double for Freud: it serves as a surrogate with which to compensate for something that is missing, a kind of prosthetic extension of life. As Nora writes, "Memory is life" (8). (Judging by the ambivalence with which he writes about it, for Nora, history's function has undergone the transformation that Freud attributes to the double, from offering reassurance to provoking disquiet.)

Nora thereby attributes an "aura" to memory, not unlike the kind Walter Benjamin attributed to original art works in his seminal essay, "The Work of Art in the Age of Mechanical Reproduction," which discusses the implications of the wide dissemination of creative work made possible by the advent of various recording and representational media. In positing history as an "always problematic and incomplete" reconstruction, Nora ascribes to history the status of the mechanically reproduced copy. History desacralizes memory, making it forever reproducible and widely accessible—and yet never quite equal to the thing it attempts to replicate. Like the identical clones in *La Cité des enfants perdus*, history always attempts, and forever fails, to track down "the original."

The value of originality is illustrated in a scene in which Krank again dresses up as Santa Claus in another doomed attempt to prompt the children he has kidnapped to have happy dreams, which he intends to steal from them by a process of electrical transference. Krank's stick-thin Santa begins lip-synching to a jolly Christmas tune played on a gramophone turntable; but when the record skips, and the refrain plays over and over, Krank's ploy is revealed to the children, like that of the melodically challenged Lina Lamont in *Singin' in the Rain* (dir. Stanley Donen and Gene Kelly; 1952), when the leading lady is shown to be lip-synching lyrics sung by a chorus girl. When the record malfunctions in *La Cité des enfants perdus*, it becomes apparent that the dreamlike scenario has been manufactured, and Krank's own duplicity and the hopelessness of his scheme become evident. He is like the Grinch who stole Christmas, failing to inspire goodwill because he lacks his own. Santa is not really singing, and the song the children hear is a mechanical reproduction, just as the Santa in the first dream was not unique. Horri-fied, the children burst into tears. (In a case of life imitating art, a similar illusion was created in the filming of this scene. As Jeunet explains in his commentary on the French DVD, the sound of the children's cries were re-created post-synchronously by adults who specialize in sounding like infants.) The children's frightened reaction comes back to haunt Krank because it is literally transferred, or downloaded, into his skull.

If multiples function as compensation for or preservation against the fear of loss, the clone copies may be read as an expression of anxiety about the potential loss of subjectivity wrought by technology. Scott Bukatman has written that "a desire for the extension of power that technologies permit is accompanied by the concomitant fear of a *loss* of power and the weakening of human control" (Bukatman 4). *La Cité des enfants perdus* plays on the ambivalence surrounding advances in biotechnology at the end of the twentieth century, including in-vitro fertilization, cloning, and stem-cell research. In the flashback to the inventor's fight with Krank, the sight of the six identical clone fetuses developing in vats adds to the eerie, nightmarish quality of the scene (prefiguring a scene in *Alien Resurrection* in which six cloned prototypes of Ripley float in similar vats). The bleak, dystopian world depicted in *Cité* would appear to harbor a dire warning about the dangers of bio-technology in the late twentieth century. Yet the "freaks" created by the inventor's experiments are closely aligned with the freak-show aesthetics of the circus, specifically that of the interwar era, and thus predate the scientific developments in cloning achieved later in the century.

The film is not as opposed to technology as it would initially appear. Although Krank's attempts to use electrical transference to harness the dreams of children to replace his own missing imaginative faculties are not successful, and although the lenses and microphones that he fashions for the Cyclops cult members are shown to be inferior to organic eyes and ears, it is not the technology that is at fault but the uses to which it is put. This is why Irvin is rescued in the lifeboat at the end of the film along with One, Miette, and the band of lost children, and why the six identical clones escape immolation while their creator (the true "original") does not. These products of biotechnology, cultured and grown in a laboratory, possess humanity where more apparently "human" creatures do not. They are rescued because they are nice guys. The conjoined twins, in contrast, are bitter and (literally) twisted, so they do not survive.

The issues of mechanical reproduction and biotechnology converge in a scene in which Irvin mischievously tells one of the identical clones that he is the original from which the other clones were minted. The clone is delighted to think that he is the model upon which all of his brothers are based. "I'm the original?!" he cries, beside himself. Irvin is manipulating the clone to get him to extract a dream from a child using Krank's mechanical contraption; the dream will then be bottled and thrown into the sea, where it will be retrieved by the diving inventor. When the clone protests that he could not possibly hook himself up to Krank's dream-extracting machine because it is forbidden, Irvin tells him, "The others wouldn't dare, but you, you can do it, because you are the original." When completing the task, the clone mutters, "It's hard to be original."

This line resonates on many levels. Most obviously, it raises the question of human individuality. The question of whether there is an indefinable human essence that cannot be reproduced in a lab is tied to the question of whether there is an indefinable filmic essence that can't be reproduced by editing or CGI, digital technology, or other means of producing special effects. "It's hard to be original" is thus also a comment about film history, about how difficult it is to make an original film, since filmmakers are always indebted to their predecessors. (Jeunet twice alludes to this meaning of the clone's statement in his commentary on the

French DVD.) This anxiety of influence is linked to a desire, by means of stylistic and technological innovation, to overthrow the "father"—or one's filmic forebears—as the French New Wave directors disparaged the lavish postwar theatrical films they disdainfully called the "cinéma de Papa," and as the New Wave's own predilection for spontaneity was passed over by the *cinéma du look* filmmakers in favor of a more rigorously controlled designer aesthetic.

Because film is a recording medium, even a fantasy film is composed of something real. But special effects—especially digital effects, which are a kind of animation—disrupt the indexical relation to the things being depicted. Irvin's prosthetic organs are not glasses and an earphone but a camera and a gramophone, symbols of the recording media. What filters through to the brain is already mediated, already a representation. The iris-closure in the film's final frames, when the boat containing One, Miette, and the rest of the children is sailing away, closely mirrors an earlier iris shot from Irvin's point of view, suggesting that the viewer is in the position of a brain in a vat and that everything we have perceived thus far is a mediated representation—in other words, a film.

In the scene where Irvin convinces one of the identical clones that he is the original, the brain is playing the part of Descartes's evil genius rather than the victim of the evil genius's deception. The brain itself becomes the agent of deception rather than the pawn (the brain's subjectivity is underscored by the shots from Irvin's point of view, distorted as though through a fisheye lens). The "brain-in-a-vat" problem compels us to consider the following questions: How can we know that our perception of the world is accurate? How do we know that the world we perceive is not simply a form of virtual reality, an illusion? How can we know that a singer is not merely lip-synching, or that a dream is not merely a bunch of electrical impulses sent through our body in a laboratory? How can we know that we are real and not some brain floating in a vat, deceived as to our own identity? How, in other words, can we know we are "originals" and not clones?

This scene also provides a direct link between the questions outlined above (notably, the philosophical question of what is real and what is illusory, or what it is that distinguishes a bunch of sensory impressions from "the real thing") and, through the camera that acts as Irvin's eyes, the theme of the work of art in the age of mechanical reproduction.

Irvin's brain in a vat prefigures the film *The Matrix* (dir. Andy and Larry Wachowski; 1999), about the illusory power of virtual reality, and is necessarily a comment on contemporary filmmaking itself, with its capacity to promote the mimetic paradox in which a high degree of artifice is required to create the greatest resemblance to reality. So, although the film evinces a nostalgia for an earlier era and a desire for a predigitalized, representational plenitude, ironically, to achieve this nostalgic look, the filmmakers must rely on the latest digital technology.

After the bottle containing the child's dream that was thrown into the sea by one of the identical clones is retrieved by the inventor, it accidentally breaks, and its contents seep out and mingle with the inventor's suppressed memories before drifting out to the port and into the houses of sleeping children. The suggestion is that dreams, like other works of the imagination, are capable of being mechanically transferred and disseminated (not one but several children awake in tears). Dreams, in many ways the most intimate expression of one's innermost desires and anxieties, are here shown to be portable and transferable—in other words, downloadable. Although the film presents dreams as signs of childhood innocence, a form of magic opposed to the cult of rationality (science and technology) and the rule of instrumental reason, it also suggests that they may be "technologically reproduced" (see Walter Benjamin). Krank's efforts are doomed to fail as long as he attempts to turn dreams into information flows—the retrieval process appears to work, but the only dreams Krank manages to "download" are nightmares. Accordingly, it is also possible to conclude that the dream of creating designer babies is similarly destined to turn into the nightmarish scenarios depicted in the film. Krank fails because he is trying to manipulate unconscious processes (which, like involuntary memory, cannot be controlled). He is trying to capture that which is elusive—in other words, to find a recipe for magic. His efforts anticipate Ripley's comment to the android Call, who crosses herself upon entering a religious chapel in *Alien Resurrection:* "You're programmed for *that?*"

Krank's inability to dream is part of his incapacity to imagine, to tell stories (the identical clones are forced to tell Krank whimsical bedtime stories in a doomed bid to inspire him to dream). He can, however, invent technological gadgets, which he gives to the Cyclops leader in return for kidnapped children. These gadgets are the lenses and microphones that the cult members use as prosthetic sensory organs. Krank is thus a manufacturer of prosthetic devices (like the army officer in *Le Bunker de la dernière rafale*). His problem, however, is that he seeks merely to extend biological perception of the world rather than to transform it through imagination.

This is a filmmaking aesthetic and ethic that is definitely not Bazinian. The film theorist André Bazin believed that the guiding principle of cinema from its inception has been "an integral realism, the recreation of the world in its own image" (Bazin 21). Referring to Bazinian realism, J. P. Telotte suggests that "[i]n the persistent concern with doubling that the science fiction and horror film genres manifest, . . . we might locate a mirror of those basic desires to which film, apparently successfully, caters" (Telotte 154). The multiple clones in *La Cité des enfants perdus* represent so many expressions of cinema's aspiration to "re-create the world in its own image"—a desire the film derides. Such a desire is expressed by the deranged leader of the Cyclops cult, who rants about a "master race" ruling the earth and urges believers to blind themselves and replace their natural vision with an unwieldy "third eye," or antiquated camera lens. By depicting the leader as a charlatan, Jeunet satirizes the belief that you can get away from the world of appearances; that there is some *être*, or being, that transcends *paraître*, or appearance, and that can dispense with it altogether.

The power-mad Cyclops cult leader tells followers to spurn the world of appearances, that it is a false world. The camera-eyes are to help them negotiate through this false world, but only so they can eventually accede to a world of essences, where appearances are no longer privileged and cameras are no longer required. The implication is that only fascist maniacs spurn appearances. According to Benjamin, it is such authoritarian demagogues who promote the aura of a work of art, its "true essence," which is antithetical to the democratizing function of technologies of mechanical reproduction. The Cyclops leader is a Dr. Caligari figure, adept at mass hypnosis and thus (following the logic of Siegfried Kracauer in *From Caligari to Hitler*) a forerunner of Hitler, with his ability to transform people into murderous zombies. The cult members are the logical outcome of instrumental reason, which reduces human beings to interchangeable, mass-produced objects. Their conformity makes them resemble one another as much as the identical clones do, and their loss of individuality is as much the product of the ideology of a "master race" as designer biotechnology is.

By means of such a hyperbolic analogy, Jeunet ridicules the idea that some forms of cinema are more authentic than others, that some get at the essence of things more than others. He is reacting against those critics who fail to see the complexity of his films' visual meaning, who interpret their visual style as a substitute for meaning rather than a form of expression in itself. In this sense, Jeunet is close to Benjamin, who, despite his ambivalence, ultimately celebrated the decline of the aura, which he saw as the exclusive preserve of the elite. Benjamin argued that to politicize art you must make it distracting. Visually speaking, *La Cité des enfants perdus* is distracting to the point of being disturbing. But at the same time, its *cinéma du look* aesthetic, with its nostalgic vision of the future, also points to the end of a political dream. According to Fredric Jameson, "Nostalgia film, consistent with postmodernist tendencies generally, seeks to generate images and simulacra of the past, thereby—in a social situation in which genuine historicity or class traditions have become enfeebled—producing something like a pseudo-past for consumption as a compensation and a substitute for, but also a displacement of, that different kind of past which has (along with active visions of the future) been a necessary component for groups of people in other situations in the projection of their praxis and the energizing of their collective project" (Jameson 137). Krank's attempts to steal the dreams of a previous generation, because his own are so ineffectual, would thus have had a distinct resonance in 1995, the year of the film's release, as the French Socialist dream came to an end when François Mitterrand yielded power to the center-right president Jacques Chirac.

The dystopian nightmare that Jeunet and Caro created with such oneiric precision (and black humor) would be continued when Jeunet struck out on his own to make *Alien Resurrection*. Yet, despite this visual and thematic continuity, not only with his next film but with the others to follow, and despite its myriad echoes of film history, *La Cité des enfants perdus* is a true original.

Uncanny Resemblances: *Alien Resurrection*

In 1997, Jeunet went to Hollywood to direct *Alien Resurrection,* the fourth film in the series that began with Ridley Scott's *Alien* (1979). *Alien Resurrection* was not only Jeunet's first film without Marc Caro (or largely without: Caro worked for three weeks on costume and production design); it was also his first experience of working for a major American studio (Twentieth-Century Fox). The relationship forged between the French director and the Hollywood dream machine was complex and fraught with ambiguities that are reflected in the film's reception and played out within the film itself.

The fourth film in the *Alien* quartet had a somewhat different reception from the other films in the series. *Alien Resurrection* did not do well at the box office in either Britain or the United States, where critical reaction, too, was much less enthusiastic than toward the previous *Alien* films. Jeunet's film was largely dismissed by English-speaking fans and critics of the previous films in the series. Its reception in France was dramatically better, where it was met with rave reviews. What is it about this film that has provoked such mixed reactions? In what follows, I will suggest that the anxieties the film elicited among critics are linked to an uncanny dread provoked not so much by the copious amounts of slime and gore as by the film's transnational identity. The multiple images of hybridity (most notably in the guise of gender ambiguity) serve as metaphors for this hard-to-place national status.

In this film, Ripley, played as ever by Sigourney Weaver, has been re-created out of a fragment of DNA retained from her body at the time of her death two hundred years earlier. But this is not the only resurrection to which *Alien Resurrection* bears witness. In addition to the resurrection of Ripley and her alien offspring, there is also that of the *Alien* series itself, which viewers were led to believe had ended when the central character plunged to her death at the end of the third film, *Alien3* (dir. David Fincher; 1992). Finally, the film also resurrects the tradition of the French filmmaker abroad.

When Jeunet went to Hollywood to film *Alien Resurrection,* he followed in the footsteps of a long line of directors who left France to make films abroad, most often in Hollywood but sometimes in Britain. The cosy partnership between French filmmakers and the English-language film industry goes back at least to 1903, when Georges Méliès established a branch of his Star-Film production company in New York and sent his brother Gaston first to Texas and then to Southern California and eventually the South Pacific to set up studios that would make Westerns and adventure films (see Méliès). After the critical and commercial failure of *Le Dernier millionnaire* (The last millionaire; 1934), René Clair went to Britain, where in 1935 he made *The Ghost Goes West* (appropriately enough, about a Scottish phantom who relocates to the United States when an American buys his castle haunt and ships it to Florida) and then *Break the News* (1938) before going to Hollywood. His Hollywood films included *The Flame of New Orleans* (1941), with Marlene Dietrich playing a French woman coming to the United States to flee a checkered past, *I Married a Witch* (1942), starring Veronica Lake (the film's publicity slogan: "She knows all about love potions . . . and lovely motions!"), *Forever and a Day* (1943), about an American in Britain, and *It Happened Tomorrow* (1944), about a reporter who can see into the future. During the Occupation, several French filmmakers fled to Hollywood, including Jean Renoir and Julien Duvivier, who made propaganda films and features, and Jacques Tourneur, whose *Cat People*, about a beautiful young émigré to the United States (played by Simone Simon, doing her best Serbian accent) on whom the "old country" exercises an atavistic attachment, achieved cult B-movie status. Truffaut, following in Clair's footsteps, made *Fahrenheit 451* in Britain in 1966; Roger Vadim made *Barbarella*, a French-Italian-American coproduction filmed in English, in 1968. These films are typical of the majority of films made by French émigré directors, many of which use fantastical means to allegorize personal or political alienation. Bertrand Tavernier's *Death Watch*, filmed in Glasgow in 1979, starred a youthful Harvey Keitel as a man who, by means of a camera implanted in his retina, secretly films an apparently dying Romy Schneider to boost the ratings of a sensationalistic "candid camera" television show. Keitel and Schneider play immigrants, he from the United States and she from France. The thematization of cultural alienation was again taken up in Luc Besson's *Léon* (1994), made in the United States, about a French hitman on the run in New York who befriends and teaches a little girl the tricks of his trade.

Janet Bergstrom has noted of the directors who worked in the United States during the Occupation that "[i]n America, these directors were always referred to, and always referred to themselves, as French" (Bergstrom 89). Such national distinctions were still maintained over fifty years later during the making of *Alien Resurrection*. In interviews, Jeunet has spoken of the differences he encountered between the Hollywood system and French production methods: "In the U.S., everything is multiplied by four. There are four times the number of fantastic people, but also four times more hopeless ones" (Campion). Most notable to Jeunet was the "the intense daily struggle, during every shot, every take," between the director's aspirations and Hollywood's insistence that the film appeal to the widest possible audience (Rouyer and Tobin 98). The Hollywood establishment seemed foreign to Jeunet, and, perhaps not surprisingly, this perception was reciprocated. Jeunet used an interpreter on the set, and there reportedly were "language difficulties" (Thomson 136)—though, where Thomson hints that the fault may have been Jeunet's, Jeunet lays blame on the interpreter, who "'didn't understand anything about working on a set, and who stood dumbly within camera range while we were shooting. What's more, since she suffered from serious migraines, she wore a gas mask to protect herself from the smoke in the studio. . . . So I learned how to say in English "tighter," "wider," "faster," and especially "shut the fuck up"'" (qtd. in Bayon 2).

The film did significantly better outside the United States, grossing $109,200,000 on its first run (compared with $47,748,000 in the United States, which was considered a failure in light of the film's $70 million budget). Abroad, the film was considered to be another big-budget American action film rather than a film directed by a Frenchman. The one exception to the film's image abroad was in France, where it was recuperated into the French cinematic tradition, having been directed by one of "their own" (see, for example, Copperman). The French press depicted Jeunet's relationship with Hollywood in terms reminiscent of David and Goliath: "*Alien Resurrection*, aside from its perfunctory plot, tells the story of the conflict between the director and his surroundings . . . with a colossal production designed to appeal to international viewers" (Bruyn). The French director's experience of estrangement is evoked in the final words of the film, uttered by Ripley when, gazing at Earth, Call asks her, "What happens now?" and she replies, "I don't know. I'm a stranger here myself," echoing the line from Nicholas Ray's *Johnny Guitar* (1954).

Jeunet may have wondered at the excesses of Hollywood, but his sense of bemusement was surpassed by the widespread perception among American critics that Jeunet's film was itself "over the top." The previous *Alien* films are considered by many to be a self-contained trilogy in relation to which the fourth stands as a superfluous addition. Why has this film been so often depicted as an unnecessary interloper, a dangerous supplement? The film's status as "superfluous" is linked at least in part to the perception that its content is characterized by excess: the film has been said to contain too many aliens, too much slime, too much horror; it is "over-the-top," "excessively gory and goo-splattered" (James). In the film, Ripley is similarly described as "superfluous": having been resurrected merely to bring the alien baby inside her to term, beyond that function, we are informed, she is "a meat by-product." Ripley herself, like the film in which she stars, is thus from the start depicted as excessive. According to the *Washington Post*, *Alien 4* "may not be the scariest movie ever made, but it certainly is the gloppiest. It's so drippy and slippery you'll feel that you're hiding in Kevin Costner's nasal passages during the filming of *Waterworld*" (Hunter). The film is also "overloaded with ideas" (Miller)—a familiar criticism of French intellectualism.

Alien Resurrection was depicted in the American press as exhibitionistic, too eager to display its graphic goo. The film is thus implicitly compared to the Betty, the renegade ship that just won't quit: at the end of the film, we see the ship's logo, a 1940s-style cheesecake pinup picture of a reclining woman. Like the Betty, the film comes back for more, stays too long, and shows too much. Kenneth Turan refers to the Betty as a "tramp freighter." *Alien Resurrection* has been criticized for leaving nothing to the imagination. Paul Tatara implicitly compares the film's display of gore to a striptease: "In *Alien Resurrection*, most of the screen time is filled with churning blobs of vein-covered guts, heads getting bashed open, and people being sucked into massive piles of entrails. And lots of people in the theater when I watched it were hootin' and hollerin' like it was the second coming of Gypsy Rose Lee" (Tatara). Where the first *Alien* was tease, revealing its secrets a little at a time and playing a game of hide and seek, *Alien Resurrection* is pornographic, getting it all out in the open. The French press dwelled on the hint of erotic attraction between Ripley and Call and on the suggestion of incest between Ripley and her alien grandchild: "The story of a loving relation-ship between a cloness and an android, which suggests that it will end under the covers," according to *L'Express* (Dufreigne); "Film lesbien," according to *L'événement* (Bruyn). The English-speaking press largely failed to pick up on these aspects on the film, or at least to write about them—with the exception of the film critic David Thomson, who, rather than discuss the film itself, devotes most of the chapter on this film in his book *The Alien Quartet* to presenting his own screenplay for a film that he would have preferred to see made: "Ripley, in a long, gold-coloured skirt, but naked above the waist, is sitting back in a chair eating figs. . . . [T]he ripeness runs down her chin and falls on the healed scar beneath her breasts" (155). Thomson's alternative *Alien Resurrection* is a soft-porn movie, a *Barbarella Does Dallas:* in a "five-star spaceship," Ripley, with her maker's "fine hand on her behavioural controls, has become a kind of space nymph, a sexual performer capable of breaking her own records at every outing" (159).

Alien Resurrection perhaps invites this kind of voyeuristic speculation because, in its very excess, the film is feminized (that is, represented as feminine). The film's status as a monstrous alien is linked inextricably to this feminization. The fourth film in the *Alien* series is considered to be lacking in relation to a norm and is often compared to its predecessors in terms that evoke classic accounts of sexual difference. For example, one critic summed up the qualities of the film thus: "'Alien' sequel looks great, if gory, but doesn't have much brains," comparing it to "a clumsy, plodding child having a big hissy fit" (Stack E1). Laura Miller calls the film "hopelessly chatty, confusing and overblown (Miller)." The word "chatty" is stereotypically feminizing (and inapt, because this film is ac-tually short on dialogue). Finally, the *Los Angeles Times* called the film "overstylized" and compared its underwater chase scene to "an Esther Williams movie" (Turan).

A brief examination of the film's themes and imagery shows that the association between inhumanness and femininity applies to Ripley and Call alike. When Call sneaks in on Ripley to attack her, Ripley stabs herself in the hand to demonstrate that she is not entirely human and can withstand bodily invasion. This scene literally prefigures the hole in a still-surviving Call's abdomen that signifies her own robotic inhuman-ity. The hole in Call's middle in turn recalls the sight of Ripley's ravaged abdomen at the beginning of the film, when the alien baby is cut from her body (figure 15). Thus, at the same time that these incisions reveal the inhumanness of these characters by demonstrating their imperviousness to ordinarily fatal, or at least painful, wounds, they also mark them as feminine, "making women" of them—which, Marjorie Garber reminds us, means to have intercourse with (Garber 93)—by suggesting the sexual organs.

Alien Resurrection thus follows in a long tradition of films showing women being cut open, which dates back to the beginnings of cinema at the turn of the twentieth century, when films of the French surgeon Eugène Doyen performing hysterectomies were shown at traveling fairs around France (Meusy 123–24). In cinematic representations of medical operations and other voyeuristic depictions of bodily incision, women have borne the brunt of the cutting. In Franju's Les Yeux sans visage (1959), a surgeon removes the faces of young women in attempts to graft them onto his disfigured daughter; in Patrice Leconte's La Fille sur le pont (The lover on the bridge; 1999), a knife thrower falls in love with his assistant, whose flesh is regularly nicked by his knives; and in The Fifth Element, the protagonist rips open the abdomen of a supernatural femme fatale to extract hidden jewels. These literal depictions of deconstruction often accompany literal or metaphorical representations of construction in which women are "created," made and unmade, usually by men—either literally, through biotechnological engineering (as in

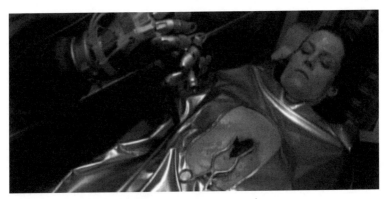

Figure 15. Ripley's operation in *Alien Resurrection*.

Marcel L'Herbier's 1924 *L'Inhumaine* and *The Fifth Element*), or figuratively, through Pygmalion-like attempts to reshape their personalities, as in *My Fair Lady* (dir. George Cukor; 1964), *Nikita* (dir. Luc Besson; 1990), and *Princesse Tam-Tam* (dir. Edmond de Gréville; 1935). Ripley in *Alien Resurrection* falls into both categories of constructed woman: the product of scientific manipulation, she also undergoes a reeducation process, albeit a highly compressed one (see Ezra, "Becoming"). The film plays with this convention by giving Ripley "inherited memories," which calls her status as a blank slate into question. When the chief science officer tells her that the utensil she is holding is called a fork, she appears to be attempting to repeat the word but says, "Fuck."

As in the three preceding films in the series, scenes of parturition abound in *Alien Resurrection* (for discussions of such imagery in this and the earlier *Alien* films, see Penley 133–34; Greenberg; Zwinger; Creed 16–30, 51, 52; and Eaton). These terrifying birth images equate feminine reproductive biology with monstrosity. Viewers need wait no longer than the film's second scene to see a team of scientists perform a caesarian section on Ripley to retrieve the slimy alien baby that has been growing inside her. One of the reviews of the film, reinforcing Elaine Showalter's observation that visual representations of medical procedures performed on women often have a somewhat pornographic function (Showalter 131–37), warns potential viewers that it contains not only nudity and profanity but "graphic surgery" (Howe). After the caesarian with which the film opens, the birth scenario is repeated practically ad infinitum and certainly ad nauseam, as we are treated to the sight of alien and half-alien creatures emerging from the ribcage first of a male human and then, dispensing with the need for human hosts, from enormous cocoons. Similar images show the pesky creatures bursting up through the floor. All of the viscous aliens sport menacingly sharp teeth, evoking none too subtly a nightmare vision of female genitalia constantly threatening to bite off a head or other protruding male member. It is almost as if the film's target audience were composed of academic viewers or film critics with a textbook grounding in psychoanalysis.

Ripley displays many stereotypically feminine character traits. After displaying such extreme vulnerability in the film's opening scenes (first as a developing clone in the shape of a naked, prepubescent girl suspended in a vat of liquid and then on the operating table), a number of subsequent behaviors reinforce her "feminine" attributes. Ripley's compassion and compulsion to protect the vulnerable are what define her as much as anything else. These traits extend back to the first *Alien* film, when the young Ripley rescues the cat Jones from the spacecraft before it self-destructs; through the second film, *Aliens,* when a more mature and more explicitly maternal Ripley goes to extreme lengths to save an orphaned little girl (who eventually addresses her protector as "Mommy") from the aliens; and in *Alien3,* when Ripley mourns the death of the little girl she saved in the earlier film, and when she caresses the alien creature who bursts from her abdomen as she is plunging to her death at the end of the film. In *Alien Resurrection,* Ripley again makes efforts to see that the vulnerable are protected, insisting, for example, on bringing the wheelchair-bound Vriess with the others as they escape.

Although these actions can be characterized as stereotypically feminine, Ripley also exhibits masculine traits. From her square jaw, chiseled features, steely gaze, husky voice, and macho swagger to her action-hero displays of weaponry and physical aggression, Ripley is a force to be reckoned with. Her gender ambiguity is summed up in the subtitle to Howe's review: "Ripley—Surely the Most 'Masculine' Heroine Ever." The holes that riddle this film are also figured, in all their sexual and gendered connotations, in the hoop through which Ripley sinks a basketball, outperforming her macho male opponent in a show of masculine prowess. This moment in the film marks the beginning of Ripley's "phallicization," her journey on the road to becoming what Carol Clover has called the "Final Girl" in horror films, or the female character whose increasing masculinization ultimately allows her to elude the killer's deadly grasp. Clover, writing before the release of David Fincher's *Alien3,* identifies Ripley as the Final Girl in the first two *Alien* films. But what about *Alien Resurrection?* In the scenes of incision, Ripley and Call both resemble victims in slasher films. But, crucially, they are both *survivors:* and, in the logic of the Final Girl, this requires them to be masculinized. Ripley survives until the end of this film, evolving from her extreme helplessness and vulnerability at the beginning, when she is splayed out on an operating table with her abdomen cut open. Ripley soon turns the tables on her captors, eventually leading them—or those who manage to survive—to safety, demonstrating superior heroism and leadership skills.

The shift in power dynamic occurs during the game of one-on-one basketball with the macho, taunting crew member Johner, who is put in his place as Ripley beats him at his own game, finally hitting him in the groin with the ball. The symbolism regarding who has the phallic upper hand is so unmistakable as to be parodic, as it is later in the film when Ripley throws a long, dismembered alien tongue to Call, literally passing her the phallic baton (figure 16). Call, played by Winona Ryder, is clearly the next generation of Clover's Final Girl, a potential victim in a horror film who survives the terrors that come her way by becoming phallicized; it is to her that the more mature Sigourney Weaver seems to be passing the reins. As one (male) reviewer put it, "Whenever they knee someone in a strategic area or even konk someone on the chin, the male members of the audience let out a squeal. Shivers run down our spine" (Dufreigne). Later in the film, Call manages to take over the Auriga's computer, helpfully named Father (the computer in the first *Alien* was called Mother). When she announces, "I've killed Father," it is hard to imagine a more overtly phallicizing Oedipal image, framed in such terms. Moreover, as Clover noted long before this film was made, the Final Girl is boyish and characterized by "smartness, gravity, competence in mechanical and other practical matters, and sexual reluctance" (Clover 204), traits that aptly characterize Call, a mechanic with a short, boyish haircut who rejects the physical advances of the men on the ship. Matters are complicated, however, by the fact that Call is not merely a girl; she is also a robot. Like Ripley, she is a hybrid creature. And it is significant that Call's moment of truth—the moment we are shown her gaping, oozing chest cavity—involves a lot of slime.

Slime figures prominently in the film as a whole. It is not a pretty picture. This excrescence is the stuff of abjection, which results, according to Julia Kristeva, from a crisis in classification, from the failure to differentiate adequately between oneself and . . . that *thing:* the abject is "that which disrupts identity, a system, an order. That which does not respect limits, positions, rules. The inbetween, the ambiguous, the hybrid" (Kristeva, *Pouvoirs* 12). Some critics have posited an identification between the monster in horror films and the female victim-protagonist (Williams; Hayward; Creed). Linda Williams writes that "in the rare instance when the cinema permits the woman's look, she not only sees a monster, she sees a monster that offers a distorted reflection of her own

Figure 16. Passing the phallic baton in *Alien Resurrection*.

image" (568). This perfectly describes Ripley in *Alien Resurrection* as she encounters the seven previous botched attempts to clone her, seven pitifully deformed creatures (all resembling Sigourney Weaver) who are literally "distorted reflection[s] of her own image." As the Betty crew members attempt to leave the alien-infested Auriga, Ripley stumbles upon a room with six vats containing the malformed results of previous attempts to clone her. These six false starts, in various stages of development, are accompanied by a seventh, living clone whose writhing body is strapped to an operating table (figure 17). This creature, played by Sigourney Weaver, is the one that most closely resembles Ripley; it is her grotesque double. Clearly suffering, the clone catches Ripley's eye, and silently implores her to kill it. Ripley not only obliges but also incinerates the six other prototypes with her large flamethrower. (This scene bears an uncanny resemblance to the flashback in *La Cité des enfants perdus* in which we see the identical clones developing in tanks in the amnesiac scientist's lab. In this way, the scene in *Alien Resurrection* is a kind of "clone" of the earlier version.)

Ripley's humane act of euthanasia (recalling a similar mercy "killing" in *Alien 3*, when Ripley pulls the plug on the broken android Bishop) prompts a male crew member to shake his head in bewilderment and muse, "Must be a chick thing." Yet it is significant that Ripley's "feminine" sensibility is expressed through a macho, hypermasculine action ("What a waste of ammo," Johner grumbles). The monstrosity that links Ripley and the suffering clone is a product of their shared

Figure 17. Clone number 7 in *Alien Resurrection*.

liminal state. The horror provoked by their encounter derives from the recognition of their similarities (the recognition of the self in the other and the other in the self).

What is most horrifying about the creatures in *Alien Resurrection* is not their disfigurement, or the abnormality of their features, but, on the contrary, their flashes of resemblance to Ripley. These moments of recognition send shivers down the spine, with the seventh clone, who bears the closest likeness to Ripley, provoking the most horror of all. This scene compels viewers to think about the fine line between Ripley and not-Ripley, or self and other. This crisis in demarcation is explicitly invoked in an earlier encounter between Call and Ripley, when Call tells Ripley that "Ellen Ripley died two hundred years ago. You're not her." Ripley then asks, "Who am I?" Call replies, "You're a thing. A construct. They grew you in a fucking lab. And now they brought it out of you." "Not all the way out," Ripley replies. "I can feel it. Behind my eyes. I can hear it moving." The question of who she is haunts Ripley, and viewers, throughout the film. Ripley is so unsettling because she is neither this nor that, neither fully human nor fully alien: she is a hybrid. Her hybridity is emblazoned across the screen at the outset in the opening title sequence, which presents an extreme close-up of a monstrous creature that is both alien and human. This gelatenous mass is unidentifiable but for the occasional tuft of hair, set of teeth, or not-quite-fully-formed eyeball protruding from a lump of quivering muscle mass: it is precisely these moments of recognition of human traits that provoke an uncanny dread.

Another uncanny moment in the film raises similar questions about what it means to be human: the moment when it is revealed that Call is not a pixieish young woman but a robot. It is significant that it is Ripley who, by reaching into Call's gaping chest cavity, first confirms Call's status as a mechanical product (mirroring Call's earlier discovery of Ripley's inhumanity after Call's knife leaves Ripley's hand unscathed). What makes this moment uncanny is not Call's mechanical nature—a clunky, metallic robot scudding around would not have the same effect—but rather the instant, albeit retrospective, recognition of her almost-humanness. Like Ripley, Call is the product of biotechnology, perhaps its logical conclusion, when the bio-logical prefix is nothing but a ghostly specter. *Alien Resurrection* depicts the progressive movement away from the body, which becomes more and more virtual, less and less "vital," even as it is perfected by means of biotechnology and information technology. This gradual disembodiment is illustrated by the shift in breeding methods used by the aliens: whereas at first they must incubate in a human body, successive generations eventually leave behind the need for human hosts. As a science officer trapped in the alien queen's lair helpfully explains to another unfortunate human likewise encased in a gelatinous alien cocoon: "At first, everything was normal. The queen laid her eggs. But then she started to change; she added a second cycle cell. This time, there is no host. There are no eggs. There is only her womb and the creature inside. That is Ripley's gift to her. A human reproductive system. She is giving birth for you, Ripley, and now she is perfect!"

As the aliens do not need to involve human hosts in their generation, so Call and her fellow robot-created "autons" have dispensed with the need for human creators. As posthuman products, Ripley and Call illustrate the family resemblance between genetic code and computer code. Jackie Stacey explicitly links Call's ability to connect herself to the ship's mainframe with Ripley's transgenerational feats of memory: "After fishing around for a connection, [Call] begins to speak as the computer, named 'Father,' giving information on the ship's power loss. . . . The separation of information from bodies that is performed here reiterates a parallel disjuncture in Ripley's evolution . . . : the dislocation of memories from subjects (Ripley has memories beyond the lived experience of her previous incarnations)" (Stacey 274–75).

The implications of this kinship between genetics and information technology are displayed in the scene set in the ship's chapel, in which Call plugs herself into the ship's computer system to comandeer it. As she enters the chapel and crosses herself before the giant crucifix, Ripley asks sardonically, "You're programmed for *that?*" This line can be understood in at least two ways. First, there is the implication that religion can be programmed, which suggests a roteness, an automatism that flies in the face of free will, an idea that is central to Christian doctrine. Second, "programming" connotes brainwashing of the kind that the Cyclops cult members appear to undergo in *La Cité des enfants perdus,* and thus constitutes a critique of organized religion. Ripley hands Call a small computerized version of the Bible, which is plugged into the ship's computer. Ripley unplugs the cable from the Bible and hands it to Call, who plugs the cable into herself. Call then ventriloquizes the computer's (Father's) instructions (as Ripley ventriloquized the child Newt's statement about monsters in the opening words of the film). Call goes on to take control of the ship, but the implication is that the ship was previously controlled (mechanically, rotely, automatically) by the Bible. Call appears to struggle with these contradictions, as she has struggled to achieve an impossible freedom of will: we learn that she broke away from her creators and burned her modem. (The faint suggestion of 1970s bra burning is evoked again later when Call overthrows Father, the ship's computer, which has both gendered and religious connotations.) Call aspires to free will, but the means of expression she adopts, religion, is shown to undermine this aspiration. This is hardly surprising, as free will is completely inimical, or alien, to the idea of artificial intelligence. According to Jean Baudrillard, "Surely the extraordinary success of artificial intelligence is attributable to the fact that it frees us from real intelligence, that by hypertrophying thought as an operational process it frees us from thought's ambiguity and from the insoluble puzzle of its relationship to the world" (Baudrillard 58).

Call's struggle to attain free will is further undermined by the fact that she yields to Ripley's will in the chapel. "Don't make me do this," she pleads with Ripley, who counters menacingly, "Don't make me make you." Yet this scene, while ostensibly showing a battle of wills between

Call and Ripley, actually underscores their similarity. Both are hybrids (Ripley is a mixture of human and alien, and although Call is pure machine, as in many sci-fi films, she exhibits character traits that are more human than those of the humans), and both are Christ figures of sorts. Call's insertion of the computer cable into her arm (while also suggesting the injection of a drug) evokes stigmata, not unlike the wound on Ripley's hand made by Call's knife and later reopened when Ripley pierces her hand on a broken metal panel in a wall. Like Ripley, Call appears to be resurrected within the film when she reports for duty alive and well after a dramatic and ostensibly fatal plunge into an alien-infested pool. Finally, Call is congratulated by Ripley at the end of the film for having "saved the Earth." But above all, their status as hybrids likens Ripley and Call to the figure of Christ, who is a hybrid par excellence (part human, part divine).

Ripley and Call, though both "posthuman," are not identical in structure or function: one is a clone, and the other is a replicant (once removed). Debbora Battaglia has proposed terms in which to distinguish between the two: "Replicants, having no necessary relationship to their originators . . . , problematize distinction, separation, and historical ruptures and displacements. . . . Clones, meanwhile, whose connection to a human original is their defining condition, problematize continuity and connection; the duplicate-original relationship foregrounds this problematic in their exchanges, which tend to produce messy human relationships" (Battaglia 507). This distinction is complicated by the fact that Ripley's hybrid status prevents her from being a clone in the strictest sense, which, by virtue of its emanation from a single source, entails the "abolition of all otherness" (Baudrillard 116). It is perhaps this that is most unsettling about Ripley: she is the clone with a difference.

Ripley and Call's ambiguous status raises issues of historical and genetic filiation. Like the amnesiac scientist's cloned creations and the minefield of Oedipal relationships in *La Cité des enfants perdus*, Ripley's biotechnological resurrection collapses the progression of generations, problematizing the idea of continuity. Ripley's status as both clone (technologically produced progeniture) and mother (host to future generations) makes her a neat emblem of the dual temporality that Jeunet deploys in his first three feature films, which harbor both the future (in their postapocalyptic settings) and the past (in their retro design features). This duality is emphasized with poignancy in the first moments of the film, when Weaver's voiceover—"My mommy always said there were no monsters. No real ones. But there are"—repeats word-for-word lines spoken in *Aliens* by the little girl to whom Ripley acted as a maternal protector, suggesting an oscillation between her roles of surrogate mother and daughter invoking an absent "mommy."

Jeunet used the same cinematographer (Darius Khondji) and art director (Jean Rabasse) on *Alien Resurrection* that he and Caro had used for *Delicatessen* and *La Cité des enfants perdus,* giving this futuristic, Hollywood sci-fi thriller a similar poetic realist feel: even the glistening slime on the alien creatures resembles the slick, wet streets of poetic realist films. The similarities in look to Jeunet's first two films (a decaying, 1930s Buck Rogers comic-book aesthetic) mean that *Alien Resurrection* evinces the same kind of vestigial memory that Ripley possesses. The scientists who cloned Ripley marvel at her capacity to "remember" things that, in her current incarnation, she has never experienced. When General Perez, the commander of the Auriga, asks a science officer how Ripley can possibly have memories, he is told that she possesses "inherited memories passed down generationally at a genetic level by the aliens, like its strength." In this, Ripley's vestigial memory mirrors that of the film itself, whose allusions to its *Alien* ancestors evoke a kind of cinematic atavism. (Jeunet originally intended to end the film with a scene set in a junkyard full of rusting spaceships from various well-known science-fiction films going back through the history of cinema but was deterred because of the exorbitant cost.) Ripley thus acts as a conduit for the disembodied "memories" of the film franchise.

Among other meanings, the series of increasingly evolved clones could suggest, perhaps jokingly, that this fourth film in the *Alien* franchise is the first to "get it right." The film contains several nods to its predecessors: as Ripley is said to have been "re-created" out of DNA extracted from her burnt body at the site of her death in the third film, so *Alien Resurrection* recycles some elements from the earlier films. These include the presence of Sigourney Weaver; the model used for the alien queen, which was borrowed from a collector who had acquired it after one of the previous films; an android with human traits, whose synthetic nature is only revealed late in the film; the signature chest-bursting moments; the aliens' sizzling blood; the band of lawless space cowboys;

and Ripley's ejection of an alien aggressor from the spaceship. The film establishes its lineage from the very beginning, with the voiceover in the opening sequence echoing lines first uttered in the second film of the series by the little girl with whom Ripley developed a maternal bond. This bond is again referred to in an early scene in *Alien Resurrection*, when Ripley is being assessed by a psychologist. When shown a crudely drawn picture of a little girl, hard-as-nails Ripley melts, her face a study in motherly love and grief. Another explicit invocation of the earlier films occurs later, as the Auriga and Betty crews flee from the aliens, when Johner asks Ripley what she did when she "ran into these things" before: she replies, "I died."

The film's allusions to the past extend even further back than the previous films in the *Alien* franchise. At the end of the director's cut on the 2–disc special edition DVD, instead of gazing out a portal of the spacecraft at the planet Earth, as in the theatrical release, Ripley and Call are shown standing on land, surveying a ruined city skyline (figure 18). As Ripley utters the words with which this version (as well as the theatrical release) concludes, "I'm a stranger here myself," we see looming from the horizon a truncated Eiffel Tower, signifying the postapocalyptic Paris that lay perhaps just outside the frame in *Delicatessen* and *La Cité des enfants perdus*. It is difficult not to read this scene as a wry comment on Jeunet's own career, with the Paris setting evoking his earlier films as well as his next film. He had already begun writing *Amélie* when he made *Alien Resurrection*, after which he returned to Paris in location and setting. The alternative ending of *Alien Resurrection* is thus a preview of Jeunet's own geographical and cinematic return to his homeland. The scene also evokes the ending of *The Planet of the Apes* (dir. Franklin J. Schaffner; 1968), in which the human fugitives, thinking they have been trapped on another planet, come upon the Statue of Liberty's torch sticking out of the sand on a deserted beach. The fact that the Statue of Liberty was a gift to the United States from France and that the film was based on the French novel *La Planète des singes*, by Pierre Boulle, further underscores the Franco-American exchange in *Alien Resurrection*. Moreover, the fact that two of the biggest Hollywood film icons of the 1990s (Sigourney Weaver and Winona Ryder) contemplate a ruined Paris throws into relief the complex relationship between the American and the French film industries.

Figure 18. Alternative ending to *Alien Resurrection*.

It is significant that the Parisian ending is the *alternative* ending, as French cinema plays the role of art-house alternative to Hollywood. However, this was not always the case. The devastation of the French landscape serves as an apt metaphor for Hollywood's effect on the French film industry, which dominated world markets until the First World War. Jeunet's vision of a postapocalyptic Paris recalls similar scenes in earlier French films such as *La Cité foudroyée* (dir. Luitz Morat; 1924), *Charleston* (dir. Jean Renoir; 1927), *La Fin du monde* (dir. Abel Gance; 1930), and Chris Marker's 1961 cult classic *La Jetée,* all of which feature Paris in ruins (see Ezra, "Apocalypse" 5–12). The world whose end is represented in these films is a world in which France dominated the global film market. Jeunet's alternative ending evokes these films and the era whose decline they lament—an era when French cinema was not simply an "alternative." Of all the horrific images in *Alien Resurrection,* this one is perhaps the most uncanny, depicting the return of the national identity repressed by Hollywood's globalizing imperative: French cinema, or the cradle of (cinematic) civilization.

The transnational can be defined as an oscillation between globalization and local or national identity—an oscillation that is reflected in the film's thematization of porous identities and liminal states and the ambivalence with which it was received by audiences. The transnational contains the national identity repressed within globalization, and the representation of this national identity produces an uncanny effect by exposing "something which ought to have been kept concealed but which has nevertheless come to light" (Freud 394). The uncanny effect that results from the oscillation between the familiar and the strange is reinforced by the scene in which Ripley ejects her alien grandchild from the spacecraft, murmering a pained "I'm sorry" as she does so. Ripley's expulsion of her alien grandchild recalls a much younger (by eighteen years in real time or two hundred years in diegetic time) Ripley's ejection of the alien from the shuttle at the end of the first *Alien* film.

However, it is not the creature's absolute difference that prompts Ripley to reject it it but rather its uncomfortable likeness to her (in this respect, Ripley's final, violent act parallels her mercy killing earlier in the film of the cloned prototype that most closely resembles her, which, while on an emotional level is an act of euthanasia, is on a structural level an attempt to preserve difference). The sadness in the empathetic gaze between Ripley and her grandchild (like that between action-Ripley and botched clone-prototype Ripley) has two causes: she feels sad because she is killing someone with whom she identifies to some extent, but she is sad also because this identification occasions the destruction of the other (figure 19). Ripley's liminal state, the divided self that makes it difficult for her to take sides and that engenders her look of identifica-tion and sorrowful compassion as she watches the life being sucked out of her grandchild, is emblematic of the the film's hybrid national status, its unsettling hard-to-placeness—in short, its transnational identity. Like Ripley, the film is "a stranger here [it]self"—assuming that "here" is everywhere. Perhaps American critics disliked the film not because it was too different but precisely because it shared too many genes with Hollywood films for comfort. Catherine Constable has argued that, at the end of *Alien Resurrection*, "[t]he final monster cannot be abjected in one swift movement because its appearance emphasizes its links to Ripley" (Constable 197). Julia Kristeva, glossing Freud's theory of the uncanny, writes in *Strangers to Ourselves:* "[T]he archaic, narcissistic self, not yet demarcated by the outside world, projects out of itself what it experiences as dangerous or unpleasant in itself, making of it an alien double, uncanny and demoniacal" (Kristeva 183). This would be the film's "Frenchness," abjected because it comprises the origins of the global dream machine, cinema's matrix.

The effect of the uncanny is much like going "home," according to Freud, who recounts a joke equating sexual intercourse with a return—

Figure 19. Ripley and alien grandchild in *Alien
Resurrection.*

for men—to the womb. In the uncanny, the homely gets repressed
and transformed into the *Unheimlich;* the comforting matrix gets transformed into all the abject images of female sexual organs in *Alien Resurrection;* and the homecomer gets transformed into a stranger, a guest
in her own home. Ripley is a host (to an alien), but she is also a guest,
a "stranger," according to the last line of the film. (The numeral 8 on
Ripley's forearm evokes the identification numerals tattooed on the arms
of Holocaust victims, who were themselves the recipients of a grotesque
brand of concentration camp "hospitality.") The debate surrounding
the concept of hospitality in the context of immigration came to a head
when Jeunet was making *Alien Resurrection,* sparked by the controversy
surrounding the ejection of a group of *sans papiers,* or undocumented
immigrants, from the Church of Saint Bernard in Paris in the summer
of 1996 (see Rosello, *Postcolonial,* esp. 1–22). In *Alien Resurrection,*
the issue of hospitality is rendered literally. The "tramp" freighter ship,
the Betty, sells human cargo to the Auriga for use in its alien-implanting
experiments. These people become guests of sorts on the ship but are
immediately turned into hosts for the breeding of aliens. When Elgyn,
the captain of the Betty, asks the Auriga's commanding officer, General
Perez, if his crew can bed down in the Auriga for a couple of nights,
Perez replies, through lemon-induced grimaces, "Mi casa es su casa."
The fact that this conventional invocation of hospitality is expressed
in Spanish is significant in a film made in Hollywood, not far from the

Mexican border, the site of some of the most acrimonious disputes over immigration in American history.

The abject results from the crossing of borders; it is what falls through the cracks. This failure to respect boundaries, whether generic (is the film sci-fi or horror?), national (is the film French or American?), gendered (is Ripley masculine or feminine?), sexual (is Ripley the alien's parent or its lover?), or biological (is Call human or android? is Ripley human or alien?) is what makes the film so unsettling to critics and makes Ripley so menacing to her fellow travelers. Like Ripley, *Alien Resurrection* is a freakish hybrid, part French and part "normal" (read "Hollywood"), part alien and part domestic product. The film's plot thus mirrors the story of its reception, with the film itself playing the role of the monstrous alien. The film's Anglo-American reception may have something to do with certain perceptions of Frenchness abroad (at least among the popular press), and the problematics of "outsiderness" and alterity informing the film's reception appear in thematic and narrative form within the film itself. Whether its critics were taking their cue, however unconsciously, from the film, or whether Jeunet's film anticipates the position that he and his film would come to occupy within the critical imaginary, cannot be determined. It is clear, however, that the film's reception demonstrates the continued relevance and potency of the science-fiction alien as a metaphor for anxieties surrounding sexual, national, and cultural difference.

The Death of an Icon: *Amélie*

After *Alien Resurrection*, Jeunet turned from what was in many ways a typically American project to what would be hailed as a quintessentially French film: *Le Fabuleux destin d'Amélie Poulain*. Within weeks of its opening in the spring of 2001, *Amélie* had broken all box-office records, and it repeated this success abroad, becoming the most successful French-language film of all time in the United States, grossing more than $150 million worldwide in its first theatrical release. The original American title, *Amélie of Montmartre* (which never really caught on), invokes the film's cultivation of "a certain idea of Paris" drawn from film history and from other visual media such as painting and photography.

Yet, in many ways, the Paris presented in the film is an alien hybrid, a disconcerting blend of the strange and the familiar: "alien" in the sense of its bearing little relation to the actual city, but also easily recognizable because of its allusions to the city's iconic status. At the heart of this hybridity is the tension between the film's use of state-of-the-art digital technology and its self-conscious quaintness, or evocation of earlier eras. Jeunet's vision of Paris would not have been possible without the aid of sophisticated digital manipulation, and it was precisely this manipulation, and the resulting lack of realism, that some critics objected to. However, amid the uproar surrounding its use of digital technology, it is easy to overlook the fact that Jeunet's film self-consciously thematizes issues raised by the modes of visual representation it deploys. In particular, the film presents a genealogy of technologies of vision, using the death of a media icon as the pretext for a meditation on the nature of iconicity.

Despite the film's huge popular and critical acclaim (or perhaps because of it), within a few months of its release, it was surrounded by controversy. Some critics chastised Jeunet for his digitally-enhanced vision of Paris, which appeared to erase, as if by magic, all traces of graffiti, crime, pollution, and social unrest. Serge Kaganski, the editor of the arts journal *Inrockuptibles,* accused the film of presenting "a vision of Paris, of France, and of the world—to say nothing of cinema itself—that is particularly reactionary and right-wing, to put it mildly," noting that "Jeunet's Paris has been carefully 'cleansed' of all ethnic, social, sexual, and cultural polysemousness" (Kaganski). A similar complaint was voiced by Philippe Lançon, in a piece entitled "Le frauduleux destin d'Amélie Poulain" (The fraudulent destiny of Amélie Poulain): "*Amélie* is successful because it transposes Eurodisney to Montmartre: same logic, same bewitched trompe-l'oeil, same cardboard cut-outs, and same sadness disguised as joy" (Lançon).

It is certainly true that the Paris in the film looks and feels little like the Paris one would actually encounter today. Gone are the bland, white-grey skies that often hang over the city, having been digitally manipulated to look at times bluer, at other times more dramatic and menacing. The film's color palette, which is dominated by yellows and ambers, giving the film a distinctly golden (indeed, almost halcyon) glow, is directly inspired by the work of the Brazilian painter Juarez Machado. Jeunet displayed reproductions of Machado's paintings on the work spaces of the set designers, costume designers, and set decorators working on the film. Machado has happily conceded that Jeunet "vampirized" his paintings "in a very intelligent way" in his use of color (Drubigny). This golden glow p̶e̶r̶meates the film, imbuing even the edgier locales and situation̶s̶ ̶w̶i̶t̶h̶ ̶a̶ ̶i̶mage of nostalgia. In Jeunet's Paris, even the sex shop is u̶n̶t̶h̶r̶e̶a̶t̶e̶n̶i̶ng, almost innocent. (Similarly, the lesbian woman ̶w̶h̶o̶ ̶e̶n̶c̶o̶u̶n̶t̶e̶rs ̶t̶h̶e̶ searching for the owner of the box of childhood ̶m̶e̶m̶o̶r̶a̶b̶i̶l̶i̶a̶ ̶s̶o̶ ̶l̶o̶n̶g̶ ̶a̶go] is made less sexually threatening, despite her ̶a̶t̶t̶e̶m̶p̶t̶ ̶t̶o̶ ̶s̶e̶d̶u̶c̶e̶ ̶A̶m̶élie, by her flapper-style marcel wave hairdo and ̶u̶n̶t̶h̶r̶e̶a̶t̶e̶n̶i̶n̶g̶—̶"̶B̶a̶d̶ ̶l̶u̶c̶k̶,̶"̶ ̶s̶he offers, holding out a cup of tea—which ̶i̶n̶v̶o̶k̶e̶s̶ ̶a̶ ̶P̶r̶o̶u̶s̶t̶i̶a̶n̶ ̶p̶a̶s̶t̶n̶e̶ss, whose potential force is domesticated ̶b̶y̶ ̶i̶t̶s̶ ̶h̶i̶s̶t̶o̶r̶i̶c̶a̶l̶ ̶d̶i̶s̶t̶a̶n̶c̶e̶.̶)

̶A̶m̶élie's Paris is in stark co̶ntrast with that presented in La Haine ̶(̶d̶i̶r̶.̶ ̶M̶a̶t̶h̶i̶e̶u̶ ̶K̶a̶s̶s̶o̶v̶i̶t̶z̶,̶ ̶1̶9̶9̶5̶)̶, which, like Amélie, was the most widely ̶d̶i̶s̶t̶r̶i̶b̶u̶t̶e̶d̶ ̶F̶r̶e̶n̶c̶h̶ ̶fi̶l̶m̶ ̶o̶f̶ its year of release. The presence of Kassovitz ̶i̶n̶ ̶t̶h̶e̶ ̶r̶o̶l̶e̶ ̶o̶f̶ ̶N̶i̶n̶o̶ ̶i̶nvokes the film he directed and with which he is ̶m̶o̶s̶t̶ ̶c̶l̶o̶s̶e̶l̶y̶ associated. La Haine is the antithesis of Amélie in its unrelen̶t̶i̶ng depiction of a Paris riven by social divisions. While Jeunet self-consciously promoted the touristic image of the City of Light, Kassovitz's film dwelled precisely on those aspects of Parisian life—crime, social exclusion, institutional racism—that Jeunet would later gloss over (or satirize—there is graffiti in Amélie, but it is an aphorism from the struggling writer Hipolito's unpublished manuscript and rather more philosophical, or at least overblown, than the standard statements scrawled on the side of buildings: "Sans toi, les émotions d'aujourd'hui ne seraient que la peau morte des émotions d'autrefois" [Without you, the emotions of today would be merely the dead skin of emotions of the past]).

The Paris in the film is, to a large extent, Amélie's vision of Paris, which is shown as if through her eyes, like the teddy-bear and rabbit-shaped clouds that people her childish reveries (figure 20). The only glimpse of anything approaching the "real" Paris is in the news footage of Princess Diana's car crash, which took place beneath the Pont de l'Alma (figure 21). This footage is a grainy, greenish hue, lit by fluorescent lights. This nontouristic image of Paris flashes briefly on the screen before disappearing, mirroring Amélie's own hasty turning off of the television

Figure 20. Childish reverie in *Amélie*.

Figure 21. Diana's crash in *Amélie*.

when she first learns of Diana's death in a news bulletin, as if she does not want to see this version of Paris. Diana's iconic status was not unlike that of Paris itself: an image packaged for the visual consumption of millions, perhaps billions, worldwide. At Amélie's local newsstand, magazines with Diana's picture on the cover are displayed next to a rack containing postcards of Paris. The connection between tourism and Diana's iconic status is reinforced by the fact that, at the time of her death, Diana was a tourist visiting Paris, and though she herself would travel no farther, her image has known no bounds. As Paul Gilroy has written:

Political institutions, even whole nations themselves, can be condensed into visual symbols. . . . Summoned by icons, even they can be sold according to the same commercial science that sells all other products. A good example is supplied by . . . discussions of the place of the British monarchy in selling the nation worldwide after the death of Princess Diana—a primary icon for both the British nation and the idea of charity itself. One message these controversies transmitted was that the meaning of nationality and the idea of national distinctiveness are now imagined to be infinitely manipulable. (Gilroy 151–52)

Diana's function as a visual symbol is at the heart of Jeunet's film, which compels viewers to consider the role of images and icons in the construction and dissemination of national identity. The "manipulability of national distinctiveness" of which Gilroy writes is illustrated further in the adventures of the traveling garden gnome. It is the garden gnome that prompts Amélie's father to take an interest in the world around him and strike out on his own voyage of discovery; and it takes all of Amélie's cunning to uproot him, as she had to apply considerable force to pry the gnome from the spot where it had been cemented to the ground. When Amélie kidnaps the lawn ornament and sends it flying around the world, the gnome (with a little help from a friend) sends back snapshots of its trips to New York City, the Kremlin, and Angkor Vat (figure 22). Paris is thus not the only city represented in two-dimensional postcard-like images. The photos of the globetrotting gnome in exotic locales seem to suggest a similar consumption of spatial and, by extension, national identity: they are the archetypical tourist scenes and condense an entire country into a single snapshot (New York for the United States, or "First World"; the Kremlin for the former Soviet Union, or "Second World"; Angkor Vat for Cambodia, or the "Third World," in this case, formerly part of French Indochina). Later, in a paranoid fantasy, Amélie imagines that her beloved Nino is kidnapped and sent around the world much like the garden gnome (figure 23). This montage sequence, which has much of the look and even the sound of Jeunet's early short film *Pas de repos pour Billy Brakko*, shows images of Istanbul (evoking the Ottoman empire), Afghanistan (evoking the British empire, which controlled Afghanistan until 1919), and Soviet tanks (evoking the cold war–era Soviet empire—also invoked in the Russian film Amélie watches on television, which features a Stalin lookalike proclaiming that "being a failure in life is an inalienable right"). This changing of the imperial guard evokes Diana to the extent that she represented the changing face of British imperialism, an emblem of the "new Britain," complete with divorce and Egyptian lover.

Whereas *Amélie* is otherwise all sweetness and light, its violent unconscious resides in the "screen" sequences: Diana's crash, Amélie's own funeral and her father's funeral (both of which she imagines watching on television), and Nino's armed kidnapping, which includes war imagery. The film also abounds in references to amputation. The owner of the

Figure 22. The garden gnome's travels in *Amélie*.

Figure 23. Nino's kidnapping in *Amélie*.

café where Amélie works, for example, lost part of her leg in a circus accident when she "fell hard" for a trapeze artist, literally and figuratively. There is also Lucien, the grocer's assistant, played by the French-Moroccan star Jamel Debbouz, whose withered arm hangs limply at his side. When the film's references to the Nouvelle Vague (1958–62), which coincided exactly with the bloody climax of the Algerian War, are seen in the light of what has been called the film's "whitewashing" or "ethnic cleansing" of Paris, which is depicted as being racially homogeneous, then we can also detect an attempt to allegorize France's truncation of its brutal colonial history. In a similar way, in *Delicatessen,* mutilation (in the figure of the butcher and various allusions to amputation) figures the cutting off of the past, which comes back to haunt in the unsettling use of television, which in a film that allegorizes the Second World War points anachronistically to the mid to late 1950s, or the period of the Algerian War. In *Amélie,* mutilation figures a denial of the present (in its depiction of Paris as the land that time forgot), which sits oddly with the extreme precision of the dates provided at the beginning and the end of the film and surrounding Diana's death.

Like *Delicatessen* and *La Cité des enfants perdus, Amélie* is difficult to situate historically. On the one hand, this is a diegetic universe devoid of cellular phones, computers, graffiti, and litter; its cafés have a timeless décor, and clothing and hairstyles are all distinctly retro. The soundtrack, which features accordion music by Yann Tiersen, bathes the whole film in the *guinguette* culture (open-air dancing and drinking establishments, usually located on riverbanks) of the early twentieth century—though, as Phil Powrie has noted, Tiersen's music contains an edge that goes against the grain of the film's nostalgic images (Powrie, "Fabulous" 150). Martin Barnier has noted other examples of this hodgepodge of historical signifiers, from the Renoir painting's reference to late nineteenth-century impressionism; Amélie's televised, horse-drawn funeral procession, which evokes the early twentieth century; and the furnishings of the grocer Collignon's apartment, which are circa 1940s (Barnier 164). Even the funfair at which Nino works seems to come from another age. As in *La Cité des enfants perdus,* the funfair in *Amélie* invokes the *fêtes foraines* (traveling fairs) that were precursors to the cinema as a form of popular entertainment, but which also provided venues for the earliest cinema showings, prior to the advent of cinemas as purpose-built structures. But more than the prehistory of cinemas, *Amélie* invokes the history of cinema per se.

Like all of Jeunet's films, *Amélie* displays a strong association with the *cinéma du look* style in its slick visuals and advertising aesthetic, as well as its attention to marginal characters. According to Sue Harris, the *cinéma du look* is characterized by "the actions of marginal or marginalized characters, people who live on the edges of society" (Harris, "Cinéma" 222). Ginette Vincendeau has pointed out that the film's adoption of the *look* style is apparent in its use of "exaggerated sounds, a saturated colour scheme, abrupt changes of scale, huge close-ups of objects or faces balanced by long takes that use intricate camera movements" (Vincendeau, "Café" 24). But *Amélie* alludes to other eras of film history as well, most notably poetic realism and the French New Wave.

Vicendeau has noted the film's "recycling" of many of the Parisian locales favored by poetic realist films of the 1930s, in particular the Canal St. Martin, where Amélie goes to skip stones (immortalized by Arletty's cries of "Atmosphère! Atmosphère!" in Marcel Carné's 1938 *Hôtel du Nord*), but also the Sacré-Coeur, the cobblestoned streets, traditional cafés, street markets, and Second Empire tenement buildings of Montmartre more generally (Vincendeau, "Café" 23). As in many poetic realist films (such as *Le Jour se lève, Le Crime de Monsieur Lange,* and *Sous les toits de Paris,* as well as *Hôtel du Nord*), *Amélie* is set in the limited confines of a relatively small *quartier,* much of the film centering around the residents of a single apartment building. Moreover, the accordion-laden musical soundtrack, as well as the Fréhel record played by the blind man in the Métro station, evokes the tradition of the *chanson populaire* closely associated with the interwar period, which featured strongly in French films of the 1930s. This era is further invoked in the televisual hallucination in which Amélie sees herself as an interwar "It Girl," complete with flapper-style outfits.

As mentioned above, the film also pasy homage to the New Wave films of the late 1950s and early 1960s. The café in which Amélie works, which provides the setting for much of the film's action, was a favored location in such New Wave classics as *A Bout de souffle* (Breathless; dir. Jean-Luc Godard, 1959) and *Cléo de 5 à 7* (Cleo from 5 to 7; dir. Agnès Varda, 1962). We are actually shown a scene from Truffaut's 1962 *Jules et Jim* (which Amélie watches at the cinema), a film that is also evoked in Jeunet's use of voiceover narration, is a mock-serious parody of documentaries and educational films. Truffaut is further invoked in *Amélie's* celebration of the streets and sights of Paris and in the many views of the city from Montmartre in particular, which featured heavily in the Antoine Doinel films. Jeunet makes the association explicit in the casting of Claire Maurier, who played Antoine Doinel's mother in Truffaut's *Les 400 Coups* (The 400 blows; 1959), as Madame Suzanne, the owner of the café where Amélie works. (There is a further, more subtle, connection between Amélie's distant father, whose neglect of his only child is in some way responsible for Amélie's later isolation, and Antoine's mother, who is implicitly blamed in Truffaut's film for allowing her own self-absorption to contribute to her son's difficulties.) However, for all its references to the films of Godard and Truffaut, Dudley Andrew has argued that, because of its high degree of artifice and meticulously storyboarded theatricality, *Amélie* ultimately departs from the rough-and-tumble spontaneity of its New Wave predecessors (Andrew 37).

In addition to its references to a range of recognizable historical periods, the film also contains a number of props that are difficult to date. As Barnier points out, "Any child growing up between the 1920s and the 1970s could have played with the little bicycles buried at the bottom of a metallic box. . . . As for Amélie's sweetheart, Nino, he pedals furiously on his 'old blue,' a timeless motor scooter" (Barnier 164). The timeless quality of the film is at odds with the temporal specificity of the opening sequence, which lists, with comical precision and in minute detail, the events that coincide with Amélie's conception on September 3, 1973 (the date, incidentally, of Jeunet's own twentieth birthday). *Amélie* thus begins at the beginning of Amélie and ends at the establishment of her union with Nino, which is marked by a similar description of surrounding events. This enfolding of the narrative of Amélie's individual life into the greater fabric of history is repeated throughout the film, in particular through the linking of Amélie's fate (the *destin* of the film's French title) to that of Diana, Princess of Wales, whose death intrudes abruptly into the film's narrative, locating the action unambiguously in the weeks surrounding her death on August 31, 1997.

Diana's death serves many functions in the film. On a narrative level, it triggers the event that will ultimately change Amélie's life and those of the people around her. Upon hearing the news of the accident on television, Amélie drops the cap of a bottle of lotion on the floor and, in bending down to retrieve it, discovers a box of childhood mementos that has lain hidden for decades. She decides to search for the owner of the box, thus embarking on her career as a fairy godmother, guardian angel, and matchmaker to the lonely and maladjusted, society's misfits. Diana's death also serves as a pretext for Amélie to gain entry into an apartment building while searching for the owner of the box by posing as a petitioner seeking to "canonize Lady Di." On an ideological level, the princess's death provokes an exchange about the nature of celebrity between Amélie and a news vendor, who remarks, "How unfortunate—for once, a princess who was young and beautiful!" to which Amélie replies, "Are you saying that it would have been less unfortunate if she had been old and ugly?" The news vendor affirms, "Of course. Just look at Mother Theresa." The nun's death, which occurred around the same time as Diana's, was all but buried by the frenzied media coverage of Diana's funeral, and the veteran charity worker was effectively replaced in the public consciousness by—or at least merged with—the princess. Diana's iconic status as the Patron Saint of Those in Need, which was consolidated by her untimely death, provides a point of identification for Amélie, whose selfless devotion to others prevents her from attending to her own happiness.

Perhaps most important, though, is Diana's status as a true icon—a *vera icon,* or Veronica figure. Her presence (if only as absence) anchors the film's relation to reality, like the indexical function that André Bazin ascribes to cinema itself, which bears the indelible imprint of that with which it has come into contact, like the "veil of Veronica pressed to the face of human suffering" (Bazin 162). This slippage between icon (quasi-mythical, larger than life) and index (guarantor of "you are there" historical contingency) informs the film's ambivalent thematization of technologies of visual representation. Although a line of dialogue—"when a finger points to the sky, only an imbecile looks at the finger itself"—would appear to warn against such dissections or demystifications of the film's signifying apparatus, the caveat serves not to deflect from but to draw attention to this apparatus.

Amélie's identification with Diana seems to fill a gap caused by a lack of close personal relationships with those around her. As a child,

Amélie appears not to receive much warmth and affection from her neurotic mother (who meets an untimely end, like all the mothers in Jeunet's films, when a suicidal Quebecois tourist lands on top of her), and she experiences so little physical contact with her physician father that her heart palpitates wildly when he examines her, leading him to believe that she has a life-threatening heart condition. Because of this mistaken diagnosis, Amélie is kept away from other children and generally deprived of contact with others. Her problem, the film strongly suggests, is a lack of intimacy. She brings those around her into contact with others but suffers from loneliness herself.

The film is filled with solitary figures on whom Amélie the matchmaker sets her sights, such as Madeleine, the concierge of Amélie's building, who idolizes her long-dead husband, giving pride of place to a huge portrait of him that is displayed prominently in her living room. Then there is Nino, the mysterious man to whom Amélie is attracted but has never met and who is something of a loner—he is never seen socializing with any other characters in the film, and he is shown in a childhood flashback being mocked and bullied by his classmates. Amélie's father, too, appears to lead a solitary existence after his wife's death, and even regular visits from Amélie fail to lift him out of his depression. Bretodeau, the owner of the box of childhood mementoes, is another lone figure, estranged from his daughter and grandson. Georgette, the hypochondriac who staffs the cigarette counter in the café where Amélie works, is self-absorbed and socially isolated; Madame Suzanne, the café owner and former circus performer, is a tragic figure weighed down by romantic disillusionment; Joseph, the paranoid ex-lover of Gina, always sits by himself; and Hipolito, the failed writer, exudes loneliness. Finally, there is Amélie's neighbor Ramond Dufayel, who is confined to his home with a rare brittle bone condition, occasioning his nickname "L'homme de verre" (the Glass Man), and who spends his life attempting to paint a perfect replica of the Renoir painting *Le Déjeuner des canotiers*. As Dufayel says of the *fille d'eau* in the painting, also referring knowingly to Amélie's not-so-secret crush on Nino, she is imagining links with an absent person instead of forging them with those around her. This is precisely the function of a media icon, with whom an imaginary relationship serves as a substitute for relations with real people—like the pornographic videos sold in the shop where Nino works, whose mechanically reproduced sex acts as a substitute for relations with real people, and like the grocer's assistant Lucien pasting the head of Diana on to the bodies of scantily clad models in a lingerie catalog.

As Amélie watches herself on television, the "real-life" media personality Frédéric Mitterrand narrates her/Diana's life story, his voiceover dripping in pathos and accompanied by swelling, sentimental music. Viewers see Amélie's own self-image projected onto the television screen in a retelling of Diana's death on a hot, summer night in France, "while on the beaches vacationers revel in the delights of the summer season, and while in Paris strolling onlookers catch a first glimpse of the traditional fireworks display." Amélie literally sees herself as Princess Diana, transported in time to another era (the clothes suggesting the late 1920s or 1930s, but with some footage evoking the First World War). The sequence reflects the two aspects of Diana's (and, in her fantasies, Amélie's) personality, at least as it was portrayed in the media. First, Amélie is a Clara Bow–style It Girl, being fêted and fawned over by photographers who follow her every move. She poses on the beach or skips stones in a self-consciously adorable parody of Amélie's habit of skipping stones in the Canal St. Martin—this is Amélie/Diana as cover girl. Then, Amélie, described as the "Marraine des Laissés-pour-compte" (Fairy godmother to the abandoned) and the "Madone des Mal-aimés" (Madonna of the outcasts), is shown doing charitable works, including pushing the Glass Man in a wheelchair on a snowy Alpine mountaintop while dressed as a Red Cross rescue worker, serving up food at a Depression-style soup kitchen, and bathing the feet of the blind man she has earlier helped across the street, upon which the man is shown gazing heavenward, surrounded by a halo of celestial light—this is Amélie/Diana as Mother Teresa (figure 24). The association among the three women is earlier reinforced when, in search of the owner of the box of childhood mementoes, Amélie poses as a petitioner seeking to canonize Diana. After Amélie/Diana's death on that fateful summer day, she is given a state funeral: "As a grief-stricken Paris looks on, millions of anonymous mourners crowd along the funeral procession, bearing silent witness to the incommensurable grief of being orphaned." Amélie, watching her "own" funeral on television, dissolves in tears of self-pity.

This televisual hallucination, in which Amélie imagines her own life embedded within history, recalls an earlier sequence in the film. As

Figure 24. Amélie as a Mother Teresa figure. |

a child, Amélie watches the news on television and imagines that she has caused the terrible tragedies she sees on the screen (train wrecks, a plane crash, etc.) by the mere fact of watching them, as she has been made to believe that she caused a car accident merely by witnessing it. As a grown woman, this intimate connection with history is taken to its logical extreme when Amélie sees herself on television, making the very history she is watching. This melding of individual imagination, collective history, and representation is characteristic of what Alison Landsberg has called "prosthetic memory": "Prosthetic memories are neither purely individual nor entirely collective but emerge at the interface of individual and collective experience. They are privately felt public memories that develop after an encounter with a mass cultural representation of the past, when new images and ideas come into contact with a person's own archive of experience. Just as prosthetic memories blur the boundary between individual and collective memory, they also complicate the distinction between memory and history" (Landsberg 19). When Amélie gives the Glass Man a video of the legendary one-legged dancer Clayton "Peg Leg" Bates tap dancing on his artificial leg, she is using one such "private memory" to inspire "privately felt" emotions in Dufayel—to say nothing of the apt image of the prosthetic limb itself (figure 25).

The precredit sequence exemplifies this blurred boundary in its melding of individual experience and historical contingency, comprising a catalog of disparate and minutely detailed personal events occurring at the same moment (the movement of glasses on a billowing tablecloth,

Figure 25. One-legged tap dancer in *Amélie*.

a fly beating its wings, a man erasing the name of a dead friend from his address book, and the conception of Amélie herself). This sequence recalls the chain-reaction set pieces so often used by Jeunet in that it privileges the minutiae of daily life, only the events depicted are linked synchronically rather than diachronically. The events shown only acquire significance in the context of an individual life, yet, taken together, they form a snapshot of a place and of a moment.

Amélie's vision of herself on screen takes to its logical conclusion the customized viewing afforded by digital recording systems, which automatically record favorite television shows and suggest others based upon these choices. Amélie's televised life story epitomizes the *personnalisation* that Gilles Lipovetsky identifies as a new form of social control (Lipovetsky 35). Such *personnalisation* enables people to insert a media icon into their own fantasies and to insert themselves into the mythology created around the icon, or at least into film footage of the icon. Lipovetsky describes "intimate confessions, proximity, authenticity" (37) as tools of mass consumerism. The film's play of proximity and distance recalls the distinction articulated by Walter Benjamin between the trace, the sign of indexical presence, and the aura or mystique of the iconic. According to Benjamin, "'The trace is the appearance of a nearness, however far removed the thing that left it behind may be. The aura is the appearance of a distance, however close the thing that calls it forth. In the trace, we gain possession of the thing; in the aura, it takes possession of us'" (qtd. in Rosen 89). Media icons are adept at providing us with occasional traces of their "real" life, which excites us because their general inaccessibility keeps us from getting too close: this combination of proximity and distance, of indexicality and aura, keeps us coming back for more. Too much aura and you end up with the queen, completely inaccessible and therefore not terribly interesting; too much indexicality and you end up with your sister or your next-door neighbor, completely accessible and therefore not terribly interesting. Combine index and aura—say, pictures of the queen in Burger King or your sister on *Big Brother*—and you have the distant proximity that is an adman's dream. It is only a short step from the enumeration of each character's idiosyncratic little sensual pleasures—piercing the skin of crème brûlée with a spoon (Amélie), cracking one's knuckles (Amélie's coworker Gina), or popping the bubbles of plastic packaging wrap (Gina's ex, Joseph)—to online bookstores' recommendation of products just for "you," based on your customer history.

Whereas Jeunet's early short *Le Bunker de la dernière rafale* plunges viewers in medias res, leaving them floating in a sea of uncertainty about the background and motivations of its characters and plot, *Amélie* more than makes up for this earlier lack of exposition, going to the opposite extreme. Not only are precise dates, locations, and even temperature and atmospheric pressure established in the voiceover that opens and closes the film, but individual characters—even minor ones—are formally presented with the explicit announcement of their idiosyncratic predilections. Jeunet first used the "likes and dislikes" conceit in the 1991 short film *Foutaises*. In *Amélie*, the device serves to introduce a wide range of characters in a short period of time, providing the illusion of well-roundedness in the absence of fuller character development. Even Amélie's cat is given this treatment, as the narrator tells us that it likes listening to stories read aloud to children. There is a tongue-in-cheek aspect to this presentational format, although it is interesting to note that the Japrisot novel *Un Long dimanche de fiançailles*, which Jeunet had set his sights on for years before finally turning it into a film in 2004, also suspends the advancement of the plot to introduce each character.

In *Amélie*, the expository style reaches its comic extreme when Amélie's parents are introduced. We are told that Amélie's mother, Amandine, dislikes the following things: the puckering effect produced on skin from prolonged contact with bath water; inadvertent physical contact with strangers, such as the accidental graze of a hand; and pillow marks left on her cheek upon waking in the morning. These dislikes, all of which are tactile, contrast with Amélie's own list of likes, which are also entirely tactile: the piercing of the crème brûlée skin, the skipping of stones on the surface of the Canal St. Martin, and the sensation of dry legumes rubbing up against her fingers dipped into a sack. It is as though the postmodern preoccupation with surface effects (according to Fredric Jameson, a key component of the *cinéma du look*) has filtered through to the characters themselves, leaving them eager to experience surfaces firsthand. In the case of Amélie's mother, the rejection of these tactile sensations confirms her neurotic, repressive nature, helpfully spelled out in the title that accompanies our first glimpse of her: "Nervous twitch, evidence of neurotic agitation." (Amandine bears both a physical and behavioral resemblance to the suicidal Aurore Interligator in *Delicatessen,* an association reinforced by Amandine's confrontation with Amélie's suicidal goldfish.)

The pseudoscientific, documentary-style titles that accompany the first shots of Amélie's parents imbue physical characteristics with significance, as though they were captions in a medical textbook. About Amélie's father, we are told: "Pinched mouth, sign of heartlessness." This comical linkage between physical traits and character traits transforms the body into a form of language, capable of expressing meaning in its materiality. Similarly, when Amélie inserts photos of herself into Nino's photo album in the form of a rebus, Nino must must attempt not to see Amélie's body as such (for example, her belly button) in order to read it (the dot in a question mark). This game of photographic hide and seek, which Mireille Rosello refers to as a kind of "playful auto-blason that Nino must read like a text, which he can neither consume nor fetishize" (Rosello, "Auto-portraits" 14), invites Nino to "read" Amélie's body at the moment that it becomes something to be seen *through,* something that is literalized by becoming a signifier. During Georgette and Joseph's sexual encounter in the lavatory, Suzanne is talking to a couple of café customers in the foreground about a celebrity whose silicone face implants exploded in cold weather: the anecdote is cruelly comic, with the underlying message that when people fetishize the body for its own sake there is the danger that this strategy will blow up in their face. The film's playfully literal renderings of figurative language similarly explore the pleasures and pitfalls of language's surface effects. When Nino finally discovers the identity of the mysterious photomat man, he is literally "turned upside down" (*bouleversé*), and when Nino leaves the café after Amélie has failed to muster the courage to speak to him, she dissolves into a cascade of water, a literal rendering of the expression "Elle s'est liquéfiée" (She turned to liquid). These expressions are literalized through the use of digital animation, but in a third case, Jeunet is content to leave things at the level of reported speech: Suzanne, recounting her romantic misfortune as a young circus performer, tells of being "dropped at the last minute" by a trapeze artist and being subsequently "floored" by the news, along with her horse, which trampled her. These scenes provide comic moments in the film and suspend (but also invoke) the tragic or violent potential that lurks within the expressions. Figurative language acts as a social bond, like folklore—but it is also a potential weapon used to distinguish those with whom one wants to associate from those one wants to reject: Gina tests Nino's honorability and moral mettle by quizzing him on French proverbs before agreeing to tell him where Amélie lives, and Dufayel and Lucien bond over derogatory rhyming games using the name of Lucien's boss, the grocer Collignon.

The film's attention to the surface effects of language is part of its examination of the play of surfaces. To Lucien's adulation of "Lady Di," Dufayel opposes his own admiration of Renoir to contrast lasting renown with vapid celebrity: "Renoir, Renoir," he shouts—but it is Pierre-Auguste the painter rather than Jean the filmmaker who is being invoked. Dudley Andrew, drawing a parallel with Jeunet's film, has argued that "impressionism . . . had bartered its social and spiritual mission for the surface effects of 'art for art's sake'" (Andrew 43). Like impressionist painting, the film explores the surface effects of art, but in this context, these surface effects fulfill their own "social and spiritual mission," thus attempting to combine postsymbolist aestheticism with some of the social concerns of realism. There is no doubt that the obsession with surfaces evinced in this film alludes to a stylistic feature of postmodern cinema, which privileges surface gloss over narrative, dramatic, or political content. Phil Powrie writes that in postmodern cinema, "images are bound together by play on the surface of meaning, much like light playing on water, and giving the same kind of instantaneous pleasure, founded in the senses rather than the intellect" (Powrie, *Jean-Jacques*

Beineix 12). This aesthetic is drawn from the imperatives of advertising. According to Fredric Jameson, in postmodern cinema, "the image—the surface sheen of a period fashion reality—is consumed, having been transformed into a visual commodity" (Jameson 130).

However, at the same time that the personalized predilections of the characters in *Amélie* invoke the marketing strategies of the society of the spectacle (and thus, perhaps inevitably, Jeunet's background in advertising), they also perform an opposing function. Unlike Proustian sensory experiences, the sensuous pleasures in *Amélie* do not serve as conduits to the past but are instead ends in themselves, anchoring their subjects in the here and now. According to Michelle Scatton-Tessier, the small pleasures promoted in the film are a form of *le petisme*, a neologism formed from the word *petit* (small) that refers to an appreciation of the tiny details of daily life in reaction to the larger forces of globalization and fears of the loss of individual identity (Scatton-Tessier 197). These little rituals create a literal adhesion to one's surroundings, allowing characters to cling to the tactile contingencies of everyday life. They thus represent a form of resistance against the vicariousness of encroaching mediatization, which promotes experience of the world by proxy.

This simultaneous attraction and repulsion toward the strategies of advertising reflects an underlying tension between the film's medium and its message. Dudley Andrew has criticized *Amélie* for leaving nothing to chance, for departing from the rough-and-tumble spontaneity of its New Wave antecedents, calling Jeunet "a filmmaker who treats his medium as a photomat" (Andrew 37–38). Tension is apparent between, on the one hand, the film's embrace of digital technology and its meticulously storyboarded creation of a bright, shiny world far removed from contingency and, on the other hand, its advocacy of unpredictability. But the film self-consciously thematizes this tension through its showcasing of technologies of representation and its use of collage techniques involving different media, which problematizes the opposition between "creative" and indexical media.

The mediatization of everyday life thematized in *Amélie* is made possible by the various technologies of representation showcased in the film. As a child, Amélie is shown using a still camera to take photos of clouds that, seen through her fanciful imagination, appear as animal shapes. When a car crashes in the street in front of her, the driver angrily accuses the little girl of having caused the accident with her camera—thus prefiguring Diana's crash, said to have been prompted by camera hounds. (The crash is evoked again when, at the cinema, Amélie informs us that she "does not like it when, in old American films, drivers don't keep their eye on the road.") Photography resurfaces in the photo booth and in the Polaroid photos of the itinerant garden gnome that Amélie has kidnapped from her father's house and sent to exotic locales around the world. Even the revenge that the child Amélie takes on the driver when she discovers he's lied to her involves the deployment of a representational technology, as Amélie fiddles with the man's TV antenna so that he misses crucial moments of a football match. The intermittent nature of this *goalus interruptus*, or disrupted broadcast, evokes the discontinuous nature of film recording and the idea of the persistence of vision.

The modern representational technology par excellence, cinema, is alluded to in the name of the Glass Man, Dufayel, which evokes the famous department store in Paris at the turn of the twentieth century that housed the largest cinema in the city. The Dufayel store became part of film legend when a significant stash of old Méliès films was discovered there in the late 1920s. The association is further reinforced when Lucien, the grocer's assistant who brings Dufayel expensive delicacies hidden in ordinary groceries (and whose name, etymologically, means light, or "Lumière"), is referred to by Dufayel as "the king of magicians," a title claimed by Méliès himself. This allusion to film history points not only to the preservation of films as a form of cultural memory but also to the archival or preservationist function of cinema itself. André Bazin famously described cinema's drive for realism as a "defense against the passage of time" (Bazin 9). Bazin believed that film, as an extension of the photograph, preserves a trace of the subject for posterity: "The photograph as such and the object in itself share a common being, after the fashion of a fingerprint" (15). Film functions as an archive of presence, of lived moments captured in their duration.

In *Amélie*, cinema's archival function is evoked primarily in the figure of Nino, the man to whom Amélie is attracted largely because he collects things somewhat manically, things that have no significance for anyone but him. These found objects—discarded photographs taken at photo booths, the laughter of strangers recorded on audiotape, and snapshots of footprints on wet cement—are all indexical artifacts. Nino is an archivist, attempting to preserve indexical traces of presence. Like Amélie when she returns the box of childhood mementos she finds under her floorboards to its original owner, Nino saves things from oblivion. The archival impulse stems from a fear of degradation of the object, the fear of finitude—in sum, the fear of death. When Amélie suggests that the man whose photographs appear in Nino's album might be "a dead person afraid of being forgotten, who uses photo booths to remind the living of what he looked like, as though he were faxing his image from beyond," Dufayel points to the revelers in the Renoir painting and remarks, "a dead person who is afraid of being forgotten. Well, in any case, these people don't have to worry. They may have been dead for a long time, but they will never be forgotten." This exchange underscores the role in painting and film of what Bazin calls the "mummy complex" (Bazin 9), or art's promise of posterity.

Yet the things that Nino archives, or preserves for posterity, can be characterised as "noise," that which was not intended for archival preservation. But in preserving it, he turns the refuse of daily life into something worth preserving. As Jacques Derrida notes, "[T]he archive, as impression, writing, prosthesis, or hypomnesiac technique in general, is not only the site of accumulation and conservation of a *past* archivable content that would exist in any case, such that, even without it, people would believe that it existed or would have existed. No, the technical structure of the *archiving* archive also determines the structure of the *archivable* archive through its coming-into-being and its relation to the future. The archival process produces as much as it records the event" (Derrida, *Mal* 34). The same could be said for celebrity, which is not only recorded but produced by the media: it is worth noting in this regard that the clock in the café where Amélie works is a "Vedette" (celebrity), as if to suggest that stardom, like all images for Bazin, "helps us to remember the subject and to preserve him from a second spiritual death" (Bazin 10).

According to Mary Ann Doane in *The Emergence of Cinematic Time*, film's archival function was the product of and a reaction to the increasing rationalization of time brought about by industrialization: "The archive is a protection against time and its inevitable entropy and corruption, but with the introduction of film as an archival process, the task becomes that of preserving time, of preserving an experience of temporality, one that was never necessarily 'lived' but emerges as the counterdream of rationalization, its agonistic underside—full presence" (Doane 223). In this sense, film came to represent (that is, to record and enact) a return to a specifically indexical, or idiosyncratic, unpredictable, and contingent, form of temporality that was perceived as waning at the time of cinema's invention. Film was embraced as a tool of nostalgia, an antidote to the transformations wrought by industrial capitalism, which, Doane notes, changed our perception of time itself "[t]hrough its rationalization and abstraction, its externalization and reification in the form of pocket watches, standardized schedules, and the organization of the work day" (221). (Even nonworking schedules have become standardized: the beggar to whom Amélie offers a coin rejects the money, saying he doesn't work Sundays.) It was through this rationalization and abstraction that time and money became equated, an equivalence evoked by the huge Omega watch on which Amélie's neighbor Dufayel has his video camera trained day and night: Omega may be the be-all and end-all in Greek letters, but it is also a brand name.

In many ways, *Amélie* seems obsessed with time. The film is littered with missed rendezvous, appointments made and broken, close-ups of clocks and watches anxiously checked. When we see footage of Diana's car crash for the first time, the film's emphasis on temporality is underscored as the narrator intones: "August 29th. In 48 hours, the destiny of Amélie Poulain will be turned upside down." This use of the date and invocation of the classic deadline structure at once situates the film historically and lends it a sense of inexorability, a fatefulness. This linear temporality, however, is seemingly at odds with the synchronicity emphasized at the beginning and end of the film, which opens and closes with a note of the date and time, accompanied by a voiceover naming various things that are taking place at that exact moment. Time is similarly suspended when Amélie pauses to calculate the number of sexual climaxes occurring in Paris at a given moment. In a sense, the film begins with a sexual climax, as all the activities enumerated in the precredit opening sequence coincide with Amélie's conception; it is possible that the film ends with another conception, after Amélie and Nino's sexual liaison, accompanied by a similar enumeration of local "atmospheric" conditions, and thus beginning the cycle all over again.

This ordering of contingency mirrors the function of cinema itself, which attempts to capture fleeting moments to withdraw them from the otherwise unstoppable march of time, but also serves to process and reorder random experience, to endow it with meaning and rescue it from oblivion, in much the same way that Amélie does when she helps a blind man (shown standing in front of a shop called Temps Libre, or "free time") down the street, narrating the various sights along the way. Cinema, with its reliance on indexical representation and its privileging of the contingent, perfectly embodies the tension between systematization and singularity. There is a moment in *Amélie* that neatly encapsulates the terms of the opposition: on a train, Amélie recites a line of poetry she has read in the struggling writer Hipolito's manuscript and which will reappear as graffiti on a wall—"Without you, the emotions of today are but the dead skin of emotions from the past"—to the train conductor, who replies, "Ticket, please."

More generally, this tension is thematized and enacted in the film by two kinds of representation: representation based on presence ("There it is"), and representation based on resemblance ("It's like this"). Representation based on presence encompasses all the indexical signs—footprints, photographs, audio recordings, and videos—but also the arrows and the pointing statue that lead Nino to the telescope through which he views Amélie holding up his lost photo album. A small boy helpfully elucidates the indexical function of the pointing statue as conduit or medium when he says to Nino: "Sir, when a finger points to the sky, only an imbecile looks at the finger." In much the same way, the Glass Man functions as a kind of medium, a transparent window or "index" directing attention to things beyond himself. *Amélie* may be of the digital age, but it continually points nostalgically to the indexical, privileging the immediacy of human contact over mediatized, iconic identification. Doane argues that, by attempting to capture fleeting, unrepeatable moments, indexical media such as photography and cinema at once resist and contribute to the systematization of time: "The technological assurance of indexicality is the guarantee of a privileged relation to chance and the contingent, whose lure would be the escape from the grasp of rationalization and its system" (Doane 10). Yet this "escape" is illusory, built into the system itself: "[T]he rationalization of time characterizing industrialization and the expansion of capitalism was accompanied by a structuring of contingency and temporality through emerging technologies of representation—a structuring that attempted to ensure their residence outside structure, to make tolerable an incessant rationalization" (11). This strategic paradox is illustrated perfectly by the video camera's nonstop recording of the clock outside Dufayel's apartment: it registers the uninterrupted, "real time" of the time piece, showing the contingency of the structure but also the structure of contingency.

The other kind of representation is based on resemblance. In addition to the mimetic arts such as representational painting and digital filmmaking, representation based on resemblance includes acts of reconstruction and *bricolage,* ranging from Dufayel's painting of a painting and the phony letter that Amélie pieces together from her concierge Madeleine's long-dead husband to the video compilations of television programs that Amélie makes for Dufayel and the newsreels and foreign-film subtitles that are doctored or personalized in Amélie's active imagination. Here, representation shades into deception, like the snapshots of the globetrotting garden gnome, the "false" picture of Paris painted by Jeunet's use of digital technology, or the disguises that Amélie dons in the photos of herself she inserts into Nino's album. These pictures of Amélie are what Mireille Rosello has called "non-identity photos" because they conceal more than they reveal (Rosello, "Auto-portraits" 14). Phil Powrie has noted, within the film, "the veiling effect of surfaces (the pane of glass she writes on to hide her face from Nino, the photograph of herself as Zorro) [and], finally, the *trompe l'œil* of Collignon's flat, where everything looks the same, but isn't, because Amélie has rigged the decor. Painterly or photographic surfaces are therefore presented to us as deceptive and full of danger" (Powrie, "Fabulous" 149). All of these signs lead one farther from the subject rather than closer to it, like the arrows that Nino follows up the steps of Montmartre, thinking they will take him to his mysterious admirer when in fact they lead him away from her, to a telescope, yet another technology of vision that mediates his view of Amélie. This dance of proximity and distance exposes the illusory potential of the index: like Bazin's Nanook, who in fact played to the camera, simulating the actions that Bazin took to be a slice of life (see Rony 111–26), the index is—if not always, then at least often—already iconic.

There is a lot of stock (archival) footage in the film: the pregnancy footage at the beginning showing Amélie's gestation; the soccer match that a young Amélie disrupts to exact revenge on the driver who made her believe that his car crash was her fault; and the tapes that Amélie gives Dufayel. Even footage that Jeunet shot is painstakingly made to convey the impression of "found" footage, such as the credit sequence of Amélie as a little girl, which has the appearance (and sound) of a home movie. This postmodern collage style is an extended version of techniques used in *Pas de repos pour Billy Brakko*. The mélange of different media points up the difficulty in maintaining an absolute dichotomy between indexical and iconic representation.

Amélie is a film that brings people together, within the diegesis and beyond. Amélie touches the lives of those around her, bringing them nearer to each other: she reunites Bretodeau with his grandson; she makes her concierge believe that her dead husband really loved her; she plays Cupid for her hypochondriacal colleague Georgette and the paranoid café patron; and she inspires her father to go out and see the world after spending years in isolation. In France, *Amélie* united left and right, with politicians from all points on the political spectrum organizing private screenings and publicly proclaiming their love of the film (Vincendeau, "Café" 22). The film's ending reinforces the idea of connection in its seemingly disparate images used to describe a particular moment in time, 11:00 AM on September 28, 1997—the beginning of Amélie and Nino's romantic coupling, or at least its public display as they ride off into the proverbial sunset. We see a taffy-pulling machine in the funfair where Nino works; a man reading a book who has an epiphany when he realizes that there are more connections in the human brain than there are atoms in the universe; the nuns of the Sacré-Coeur practicing their tennis backhand; and the temperature and levels of humidity and atmospheric pressure. All these images illustrate the idea of connection or engagement (not to mention, as Arletty in *L'Hôtel du nord* puts it, "atmosphère").

The contact that *Amélie* privileges is allied with contingency not only etymologically, in its celebration of characters who reach out and "touch" someone), but semantically as well. The film seems to be against iterability and iconicity. When Dufayel expresses disapproval with Lucien for his infatuation with Lady Di, he explicitly invokes Pierre-Auguste Renoir in opposition to the cover girl, apparently contrasting weighty, serious renown with vapid celebrity. But, by the same token, as long as the Glass Man makes endless copies of his painting, he will never "get a life." Yet it is he who opens Amélie up to the contingency of singular events, exhorting his young friend, on videotape, to "take a chance." When Amélie and Nino finally kiss, Dufayel tells Lucien, who has been filming them, to turn the camera away, thus underscoring the literal obscenity of the act, its need to occur offstage (*ob-scene*). Yet Dufayel's advocacy of immediacy is undermined somewhat by the fact that he communicates with Amélie by video. Dufayel attempts to preserve the absolute, unrepresentable singularity of the encounter by refusing to mediate it or to turn it into a media event, but he cannot prevent the encounter itself from being utterly iconic. Like the fifteen sexual climaxes she "observes," Amélie's decision to "take a chance" invokes the wholly licit and nonfortuitous pleasures of the classic film plot. Each of the fifteen orgasms occurring in Paris at a given moment may be spontaneous, but together they lay down a law of averages, creating an actuarial basis for the prediction of other cinematic climaxes. As Doane oberves, "In line with the logic of statistics, the cinema has worked to confirm the legibility of the contingent" (208). So at the end of the film, even though it is the video that brings the hitherto star-crossed lovers together, the sheer predictability of their union, the "fabulous" storybook fulfillment of Amélie's *destin,* recalls the ending of countless Hollywood films. The film's resistance against iterability reiterates the indexical drive of the cinematic medium. In turn, Amélie herself has become an endlessly reiterated icon, one whose story is reassuringly familiar and whose face has been reproduced all over the world. Although the film appears to endorse iconoclasm, it ultimately (if knowingly) reproduces a cliché.

Screen Memories: *Un Long dimanche de fiançailles*

Although Jeunet's next film, *Un Long dimanche de fiançailles,* was not finished until 2004, he had conceived the project some fifteen years earlier, and plans to make the film were well under way when he made *Amélie.* The films were linked in the public perception by the presence of Audrey Tautou in the starring roles and by their use of voiceover narration and authentic and re-created newsreel footage for largely comic effect (prompting the oft repeated comment that *Un Long dimanche de fiançailles* could alternatively be called *Amélie Goes to War*), but what links the two films above all else is the fact that they both inspired national debates about the definition of Frenchness: *Amélie* in its depiction of a Paris that did not reflect "the real France," which was a lot more multicultural than the film suggested; and *Un Long dimanche de fiançailles* by virtue of the national identity of the film itself. This national identity was the subject of a protracted and well-publicized court battle to determine if the film was eligible to benefit from state subsidies for domestically produced French films, which the film's producers ultimately lost ("Film Ruled"). Headlines blared, *"Un Long dimanche de fiançailles* Is No Longer French!" (Cuyer).

As Graeme Hayes and Martin O'Shaugnessy have pointed out, this ruling was more a question of economics than of a concern for the French *exception culturelle:* "Given the multiplicity of levels on which the national identity of a film might be located—the source, the setting, the aesthetic strategies and contexts, the nationality of the director, audience analysis—the tribunal's decision simply asks us to follow the money" (Hayes and O'Shaugnessy 6). Symbolically stripped of its French nationality, the film was barred from competing at Cannes because, having opened in the United States in November 2004, it was deemed to have been screened "outside its country of origin" before the festival—the country of origin being France. For the purposes of the Cannes festival, the film was too French: if it had been deemed American, there would have been no problem with showing it outside of France. *Un Long dimanche de fiançailles* was thus relegated to a cinematic No Man's Land, like the soldiers depicted in the film. Sue Harris has pointed out that the controversy surrounding the film's national identity represented "[c]urious times for a film whose literary and historical heritage is so distinctly French" (Harris, Review 78). *Un Long dimanche de fiançailles* is indeed very "French," not only because it is based on Sébastien Japrisot's bestselling French novel and invokes canonical French literary figures such as Baudelaire, Apollinaire, and Maupassant, and not only because it treats the subject of the First World War, which played such a major role in the French political and cultural imagination of the twentieth century, but also by virtue of its loving depiction of the major touristic sites of Paris as well as of key French provincial locations. But paradoxically, it is in its emphasis on sites of "Frenchness" that the film is at its most transnational: these touristic sites act as screen memories to divert our gaze from the border zones of contested national identity.

Un Long dimanche de fiançailles represents a departure for Jeunet;

whereas several of his earlier films thematized historical trauma on a latent level, this film brings the issue out in the open. In a logical extension of the earlier films' metaphorical allusions to psychic wounding and disengagement, *Un Long dimanche de fiançailles* deals with physical wounding and dismemberment—the opening frames show a truncated Christ dangling askew from a crucifix. The plot revolves around five soldiers who are sentenced to death for committing self-multilation in a bid to be sent home from the front. Mathilde, the fiancée of one of the soldiers, refuses to believe that her beloved Manech has been killed and sets out to find the truth, criss-crossing the country in spite of her disability, a limp caused by childhood polio.

Un Long dimanche de fiançailles is in many ways a French heritage film, conforming to the genre's predilection for costume dramas based on popular literary classics (although Japrisot's novel, published in 1991, has not had the chance to stand the test of time, it became an instant bestseller and was received with the kind of gravitas usually reserved for war epics). As Ginette Vincendeau describes them, "Heritage films are shot with high budgets and production values by A-list directors and they use stars, polished lighting and camerawork, many changes of décor and extras, well-researched interior designs, and classical or classical-inspired music. Their lavish mise-en-scène typically displays the bourgeoisie or aristocracy" (Vincendeau, *Film* xviii). Although heritage films are often dismissed for presenting a rose-tinted view of history, Vincendeau points out that French examples of the genre tend to be more critical of the past than do their British counterparts (xix–xx). Jeunet's film displays features of the British and the French heritage film: while painting an idealized picture of life in interwar France, it also presents an unflinching view of the First World War and a caustic condemnation of the callousness of many of those in power. Jeunet has said that he made this film to preserve the memory of the soldiers who fought in the First World War, as the last of them were dying. Just as Mathilde attempts to reconstruct the past based on letters, mementos, and personal recollections, Jeunet strives to bring an era back to life through the use of authentic and artificial archival footage.

According to many historians, the First World War was the defining instance of historical trauma in the modern era. Jay Winter has pointed out that "the notion of traumatic memory is by and large a product of

World War I" (Winter). Hayden White calls the First World War one of the "holocaustal" events of the twentieth century, which "cannot be simply forgotten and put out of mind, but neither can they be adequately remembered; which is to say, clearly and unambiguously identified as to their meaning and contextualized in the group memory in such a way as to reduce the shadow they cast over the group's capacities to go into its present and envision a future free of their debilitating effects" (White 20). Because it could not be adequately articulated or represented after the fact, the war haunted those who endured it, either as soldiers or family and friends awaiting the return of loved ones (many of whom were never seen again or were virtually unrecognizable when they did return). This haunting was silent and all-consuming. Examining the idea that survivors of the war were unable to communicate their experiences afterwards, Winter notes that "after the shock of World War I many men and women had grown 'not richer but poorer in communicable experience.' Their memories were not on the surface but went underground. Alongside the public commemorations, or rather in their shadow, men and women lived out lives that were overwhelmed by memory" (Winter).

This double bind of the overwhelming but unspoken memory informs the film's obsession with memory. The film consists largely of people relating first- or second- or even thirdhand accounts of sightings of Manech and his comrades. What Winter calls the "underground" quality of this memory is illustrated by Mathilde's painstaking attempts to build a picture of the past that serves as an alternative to the official version of events that she suspects to be—and which ultimately turns out to be—untrue. The countermemory that gradually emerges is pieced together from people's partial recollections, which function like the film's repetition of the scene in which a fire starts in Mathilde's room: the second time it is shown, we (and Mathilde) have a different perspective on the incident. This double take functions as a metaphor for the structure of history, which is composed of several partial and incomplete accounts of an event. At the heart of all these recollections, in the eye of the storm, is their object, Manech, who has no memory at all. In a sense, Manech is resurrected at the end of the film (like Ripley in *Alien Resurrection*), after Mathilde is told on several occasions, by military personnel and by her concerned family, that he is dead. Like the soldiers killed on the battlefield who rise from the dead at the end of Abel Gance's *J'Accuse* (1919), Manech is reanimated, but as a hollow shell of his former self. It is this void at the center of the film that the multiple accounts and recollections are there to compensate for. Like the inventor in *La Cité des enfants perdus*, Manech triggers the events of the film but is unable to recall his actions (he appears to be the only character in the film who does not recall what happened during the war). The implication in both films is that traumatic memory is not compatible with survival: the inventor finally remembers but dies, while Manech survives but has no memory.

Mathilde strives to fill the void by reconstructing the past that Manech has forgotten. The lines of communication that forge links with the past are figured in the numerous allusions to *fils* (threads, lines, or wires) throughout the film. The film opens on a dank, gloomy scene in the trenches, as five soldiers are led through the mud in the driving rain. As they walk through the narrow trench, the officer leading them calls out periodically, "Attention au fil" (Watch out for the wire) (figure 26). This warning provides a recurring motif as well as a *fil conducteur,* or guiding thread, through the film's labyrinthian story. The *fils* are the networks of communication that link characters to each other and to their historical period: the letters, telephone calls, photographs, newsreels, early films (authentic and re-created), telegraphy, and secret codes that feature in the plot as well as the modes of transportation that give rise to the deadly operations of war but that also bring people together. The *fils* are the links in the chain of command, desire, and memory. They are the ties that bind, in terms of affection and affliction, eros and thanatos: Manech and Mathilde's love is described more than once as a "fil," and Manech feels Mathilde's heart beating in his hand "like Morse code." After Manech wounds his hand, the narrator tells us that "Every time his wound throbs, Manech feels Mathilde's heart pulsating in the palm of his hand, and each beat brings him closer to her." But the narrator tells us that if the *fil* does not lead Mathilde to Manech, she is prepared to hang herself with it, adding: "Since the notification of his death, she clings obstinately to her intuition as though to a taut wire." The plot is driven by the question of whether the film will ultimately be a tragedy (ending with the death of Manech and, as the last quote strongly suggests, Mathilde as well) or a comedy in the classical sense (ending with a marriage).

Figure 26. Wire in the trenches in *Un Long dimanche de fiançailles.*

The drive to reconstruct a past that has remained inaccessible is reinforced by the profusion of codes and the emphasis on decipherment in the film, which evoke some of the techniques used in wartime espionage, underscoring the fact that the French were the most effective cryptanalysts of the First World War, with the most advanced codebreaking practices in Europe (Singh 104). Mathilde's own sleuthing efforts (complete with the exaggeration of her infirmity by means of an unnecessary wheelchair) are aided by her employment of the private detective Germain Pire, a plot device that lends the story the atmosphere of crime fiction. Anton Kaes has written of the way that the trench mentality pervaded civilian life in interwar Europe, leading to an atmosphere of paranoia and a preoccupation with crime and the search for the hidden enemy (Kaes). In *Un Long dimanche de fiançailles,* the "crime" in question is committed by the French War Ministry, a result of mistaken identity, callous disregard for human life, and a coverup. (In some ways, Mathilde seems to be struggling with her own private Dreyfus Affair, with Tina Lombardi as a would-be Emile Zola, accusing the guilty but going further than Zola's "J'Accuse" by exacting a particular brand of vengence: murder.)

Perhaps the most literal code that requires breaking in the film is the inscription "MMM," which remains a mystery until Manech reveals its meaning when he shouts, "Manech aime Mathilde! Mathilde aime Manech!" (Manech loves Mathilde! Mathilde loves Manech!) atop a cliff on which he has just carved the letters. To understand the code, it is necessary to hear the second letter as the word it sounds like (*aime*) instead of reading it as written. This auditory dimension gives the lovers' secret language a poetic weight, because the code can only be cracked if the letters are read aloud, as poetry was originally meant to be. The phonetic kernel of this literal declaration of love goes against the grain of the visual poetry popularized by Apollinaire around the time of the First World War (in which the poet died), which turned audiences of lyrics into viewers of poetic paintings. We must see-but-not-see the second of the three M's (that is, we must stop "seeing" the letter in order to "hear" the love—*aime*—it voices), just as Mathilde must learn to overlook the other words surrounding the secret message in the coded letter about the price of fertilizer (and just as the German woman in the café erases most of the words on the chalkboard menu to send a signal to Mathilde). Similarly, Mathilde must learn to disregard the false starts and inaccurate information provided in the film's many partial or misremembered accounts of the war. Seeing, the film suggests, involves a degree of blindness, just as surviving traumatic events requires a certain amount of forgetting.

The constant and almost obsessive revisiting and revision of past events within the film performs a working-through and thus a kind of resolution of the trauma of the war. But at the same time, many aspects of the film pose an obstacle to this resolution: the emphasis on the partiality and incompleteness of individual accounts of the war, the disparity between the official version of events and the countermemory that Mathilde laboriously constructs, and the conclusion that is at once neatly sewn up (the lovers are reunited) and inconclusive (Manech has no memory of Mathilde). It is highly significant that the person who has experienced the events that Mathilde has tried so hard to reconstruct cannot remember them and thus cannot process or work through them. The memories of others act as a substitute for Manech's lost memory in a peculiar version of "prosthetic memory." Although Manech's predicament seems to emblematize the structural opposite of prosthetic memory in that, as the one who experienced the events, he remembers nothing, his condition (and, by extension, the unspeakable trauma of the war) is actually the condition of possibility of prosthetic memory itself. According to Alison Landsberg, "[P]rosthetic memories, like an artificial limb, often mark a trauma" (Landsberg 20).

Un Long dimanche de fiançailles illustrates the function of prosthetic memories in its use of stock footage and sequences filmed by
Jeunet that are made to look like stock footage, which at once signal a
trauma and divert the gaze from it. The "newsreels" in the film are the
opposite of historical fiction or docudrama, which fictionalizes historical events: these short films appear to lend historical authenticity to a
work of fiction. Jeunet embeds (post)modernist elements—the use of
archival and pseudoarchival footage that blurs the distinction between
history and fiction—within a traditional romantic narrative structure.
This often tongue-in-cheek fusing of fact and fiction would be what
Hayden White calls a "modernist technique of representation," which
"provides the possibility of de-fetishizing both events and the fantasy
accounts of them which deny the threat they pose, in the very process of
pretending to represent them realistically. This de-fetishizing can then
clear the way for that process of mourning which alone can relieve the
'burden of history.'" (White 32).

Just as the film depicts the suppression of traumatic events through
the imposition of a factually inaccurate official version of events, it suggests the merging of individual memory and history through the use of
archival footage (for example, Mathilde's bout of polio is represented by,
and becomes equatable with, scientific advances in fighting the disease;
Elodie and Benjamin Gordes's private dream of visiting the seaside takes
the shape of *actualité* footage of a public beach). Like the footage of the
car crash that killed Princess Diana in *Amélie,* these sequences provide
indexical linkage to the historical era depicted in the film, but they
also undermine the pretense to indexical representation in their lack of
distinction between archival films and films made to look like archival
films. The content of the stock footage is at times contradicted by the
diegetic events surrounding it. For example, as Mathilde masturbates in
a display of sexual self-sufficiency, we see a sequence made to look like
a scene from a serial melodrama of the kind popularized by Feuillade
during the First World War, in which Mathilde plays a coy seduction
game of cat and mouse with her suitor while a voiceover announces,
"Mathilde never needs to pursue her fantasies to the end before she
is carried away by pleasure." Similarly, the stock footage of the seaside
resort is a cruel reminder that Elodie and Benjamin will never achieve
their dream of seeing the sea; and the newsreel footage of polio microbes

seen through a microscope belies the fact that science has not been able to cure Mathilde's polio.

Although the nine *actualité* films shown throughout *Un Long diman-che de fiançailles* appear to be randomly chosen, they are linked by the common threads of *eros* (Mathilde's birth, with her parents united in love and pride; Mathilde's serial-film seduction; Elodie Gordes's dream of a romantic seaside vacation with her husband) and *thanatos* (Mathilde's parents' death in a bus accident; maritime emergencies; a soldier's execution; a major flood in Paris; polio; and Tina Lombardi's beheading). Tina Lombardi, a prostitute whose lover, Ange Bassignano, is one of the five soldiers condemned to die in No Man's Land, unites the two themes because she commits murder by means of sexual seduction and dies for love, having embarked on a quest to kill those officials responsible for her lover's death. In this, the character bears a striking resemblance to Irma in Guy de Maupassant's story "Le lit 29" (1884), who, during the Franco-Prussian War, considers it her patriotic duty to infect as many Prussian soldiers as possible with syphilis (with the notable difference that it is the French, not German, military officers whom Tina kills). Mathilde and Tina are at more than one point said to be conducting parallel investigations, so their lives are paralleled, too. The women are explicitly compared when Mathilde says the reason she would not exact the kind of vengeance that Tina has is that she "would be too afraid," not because she is morally repelled by the other woman's acts of murder. The outcomes of their lives, however, are opposed: Mathilde ends the film reunited with her lover, while Tina ends up dead. This opposition is illustrated starkly in the faux-archival vignettes that feature each of the women: Mathilde as the object of seduction (in the fantasy film serial), and Tina as the subject of a beheading (in a reconstructed *actualité* film made to look like footage of the last state execution in France, when Eugen Weidmann was guillotined in 1939) (figure 27).

The comparison between the two women is further reinforced by the parallels between Tina's preparations for her execution and Mathilde's preparations for her reunion with Manech at the end of the film: Mathilde applies a touch of makeup and decides to wear a white dress "pour la fraîchaur" (for a crisp, fresh look), the narrator tells us, whereas Tina frets about getting her hair cut. We see it shorn, St. Joan–style, for her beheading, while her coarse, drab grey clothes contrast with Mathilde's

Figure 27. Tina Lombardi's execution in
Un Long dimanche de fiançailles.

light, summery dress. Moreover, these characters' final scenes differ in
their articulation of each woman's "viewing position": whereas Tina is
pure object, filmed in extreme long shot and literally unable to return
the gaze as she is decapitated, Mathilde's final scene, and that of the
film, ends as she sits staring at Manech (who, unperturbed, continues
going about his business), as the voiceover repeats, "She looks at him.
Looks at him. Looks at him."

Eroticism and death are again linked when Major Lavrouye uses the
paper bearing Manech's stay of execution to adjust his magnifying glass in
order to examine postcards of naked women. The official ignores the stay
of execution, thus showing a callous disregard for human life, preferring
literally to focus on the erotic photographs instead. This deflection of
the deadly horrors of war onto eroticism is mirrored on a more general
level in the film's emphasis on romantic relationships. Elodie Gordes,
Mathilde, and Tina comprise a triptych of feminine sexual roles, with
Mathilde the almost eternal fiancée and Tina Lombardi the prostitute
ostensibly at opposite ends of the spectrum of social respectability and,

somewhere in between, Elodie, the faithful wife and mother who, at the urging of her husband Bastoche, sleeps with his best friend in an attempt to conceive a child and thus get Bastoche discharged from the army. A comparable triad is formed in *Amélie,* with Princess Diana emblematizing the fun-loving It Girl, Mother Theresa the selfless, nurturing saint, and Amélie vacillating between the two. In each case, the three women who make up the triangle embody three alternatives in marital status: Mathilde is engaged, Elodie is a wife and mother, and Tina is a prostitute; while Amélie is single, Diana divorced, and Mother Theresa a celibate nun. At the same time, the three women in each film are of three different nationalities: Mathilde is French, Elodie Gordes is a Polish immigrant, and Tina Lombardi is Corsican; while Amélie is French; Mother Teresa is Albanian-Macedonian, and Diana is British.

In both films, female bodies (implicit in the women's association with their sexual/marital status) are represented as sites of culture onto which various tensions and desires surrounding national identity are projected. In *Un Long dimanche de fiançailles,* Major Lavrouye's postcards objectify human beings in a similar manner to war itself, reducing people to their corporeal existence (figure 28). In this objectification process, gender roles are magnified to become defining characteristics: men at war are reduced to agonistic bodies, while sexually objectified women are reduced to erotic bodies. The titillating postcards the major views construct women's bodies as touristic sites (to be gazed at

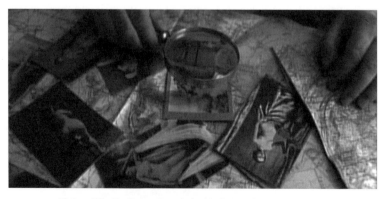

Figure 28. Erotic postcards in *Un Long dimanche de fiançailles.*

or "visited" briefly, like the Eiffel Tower, or like the Corsican brothels Germain Pire visits in the name of "research"), thus implicitly linking the commodification of women in prostitution to the commodification of national identities in mass tourism. Paul Virilio has written with regard to pinup posters and erotic postcards that "[t]he leer that the conquering soldier casts on a woman's now-distant body is the same as that which he directs at a land turned into desert by war. It is also a direct antecedent of the cinematic voyeurism with which a director films the star as one does a landscape, with its lakes, contours, and valleys" (Virilio 22). Virilio suggests that a similar sense of "visual pleasure," to use Laura Mulvey's term, is cultivated in the sight of women's bodies and in beautiful landscapes of the kind shown in heritage films. These images function as cinematic attractions (like the dazzling tricks and visual displays in the earliest films), arresting the viewer's gaze and interrupting the narrative flow of the film. Just as sex deflects from death in the film, so the dazzling landscapes deflect from the more troubling sites of national and international tension. Although the film has drawn attention for its unflinching depiction of trench warfare (which was inspired by Steven Spielberg's *Saving Private Ryan*), it was above all noted for its painstaking re-creation of early 1920s France. Jeunet seems to have shared Mathilde's drive to reconstruct the past, and this is reflected in the production design's extraordinary attention to detail.

Many of these details, however, do not come from Japrisot's novel. The home of the aunt and uncle with whom Mathilde lives in the film is in Brittany. In Japrisot's novel, however, Mathilde lives with her parents in a vacation home in Cap-Breton in the southwest of France, which is where, as a child, she meets Manech. The novel explains of Manech: "He was born in Cap-Breton, from where one can see Biarritz, but since geography was not the strong suit of those in the armed forces, the men in Manech's unit thought he came from Brittany. He had given up correcting them on his very first day" (Japrisot 23). In the novel, Manech's family name is Etchevery, which is Basque, but in Jeunet's film, Manech's family name is Langonnet, after a village in Brittany. In both the novel and the film, Manech's name literally anchors him to his place of birth, but the symbolic functions of these locations differ. In the cultural shorthand used by Jeunet, Brittany—the land of majestic coastal views, crêpes, and good-natured, down-to-earth locals—presents a greater geographical contrast to Corsica, the homeland of Ange Bassignano and Tina Lombardi, than does the Basque country in the southwest of France. The idea of separatism associated with the Basque region (and therefore with Mathilde and Manech in the novel) is transferred in the film to Ange and Tina by way of Corsica. They are the enfants terribles of the story, the transgressive figures. In Japrisot's novel, Ange and Tina come from Marseilles, and the change to Corsica adds a certain exoticism to the film. In contrast to the modernity that Paris represents, Corsica is depicted as the land that time forgot, its customs even quainter and more archaic than those of Brittany or the farm in the Dordoigne called "Au bout du monde" (The end of the world). The burnt-ochre landscape is lovingly filmed, the small villages digitally manipulated to enhance their Old World charm: perhaps more than any other location in the film, Corsica conveys the impression of an advertisement sponsored by the tourist board. But Corsica is depicted as sufficiently distinct from metropolitan France as to problematize its Frenchness. This France, in other words, is so *profonde* that it is practically subterranean. Germain Pire, the private detective hired by Mathilde to find information about Manech's fate, is shunned by the closed community: despite his deep southern French accent, he appears too suspiciously northern, or urban, to the villagers. When Ange Bassignano, about to be shot, screams that he's "not even French," the issue of French identity is brought to the fore. Corsica is technically a territorial collective and is treated legally and administratively as part of metropolitan France. Although it is separated geographically from France by the Ligurian Sea, it is not considered to be an "overseas" territory or department. The Corsican flag shows a picture of a Moor's head, the emblem of Corsican independence. Throughout Corsican history, there has been an uneasy relationship between the island's Frenchness (Napolean was a native of Corsica) and its struggle for independence.

La Plus Grande France (Greater France, the informal name of the French colonial empire) is again invoked in the film's brief references to the colonial troops who fought in the war. Near the beginning of the film, we see a group of African soldiers—*tirailleurs sénégalais*, or West African colonial conscripts—march across the screen. This nod to the colonial troops is echoed near the end of the film, when Célestin Poux tells Mathilde and her aunt and uncle how he made the money to buy his motorcycle by trading woolen scarves and mittens to West African soldiers in return for gold fillings they had extracted from the mouths of dead Germans (evoking the gold-mining industry that was a mainstay of colonial exploitation in West Africa). These allusions to empire are fleeting, but, combined with the film's depiction of Corsica, they evoke some of the people and places at the margins of French national identity.

Brittany, in contrast, is depicted as the French heartland, its traditions enfolded into the national *patrimoine*. Brittany anchors the film's national distinctiveness and serves as a hub around which radiate a series of contrasts. First, with its clifftop locations and aerial views, Brittany functions as the structural opposite of the trenches of the Somme. The trenches are wet, lugubrious, and muddy (changed from snowy in the novel), while the Breton countryside, with the exception of a scene set in the rain and a brief shot of Mathilde playing the tuba against a background of grey clouds, is largely (and uncharacteristically) sundrenched. Mathilde lives with her aunt and uncle in a charming thatched-roof cottage, the family takes walks along the cliffs, and Mathilde hobbles, to catch a last glimpse of Manech as he is driven off to war, through the tall grasses that are (again, improbably) dried out by the sun. Towering above the Breton landscape is the lighthouse that acts as a veritable monument to Mathilde and Manech's love, complete with swelling romantic music and sweeping crane shots. This lighthouse could not be more different from the dark and foreboding structure looming out of the blackness in *La Cité des enfants perdus*. It is to the lighthouse in Brittany that Mathilde goes on her own, near the beginning of the film, to forge her determination not to accept the official story of Manech's fate. It is here that Manech and Mathilde play as children, and here, in a playful evocation of the lighthouse's phallic imagery, that their mutual affection first takes a sexual turn.

As a counterpoint to the radiant and expansive Breton landscape, the film presents a series of equally sparkling, but bustling and urban, Parisian locales. The obvious parallel to the lighthouse would be the Eiffel Tower, which serves as the imposing backdrop to a scene of domestic bliss for Elodie and Benjamin Gordes (figure 29). Built as a symbol of France's industrial and technological prowess for the 1889 World's Fair, by the early twentieth century the Eiffel Tower had already become a tourist icon and a symbol of national identity that France projected to

Figure 29. Beneath the Eiffel Tower in
Un Long dimanche de fiançailles.

the world. The exploding fireworks in the background, moreover, suggest
that the scene is taking place during the *fête nationale* of July 14, the
national celebration of French republicanism. Perhaps above all else,
the Eiffel Tower is the iconic symbol of Paris itself, and Jeunet's carefully
constructed, digitally enhanced depiction of it gives the impression of a
filmic postcard—one of several in *Un Long dimanche de fiançailles.*

The busy, noisy Paris scenes contrast with the serenity of provincial
life depicted in the film. Mathilde is an outsider in Paris on a mission,
and she does not succumb to the city's charms. Although she covers a
lot of ground and visits many different Parisian sites, she is anything but
what Baudelaire described as a *flâneur:* she is not trying to kill time but
trying to bring it back to life. In fact, she is the opposite of a *flâneur* in
many respects. She limps rather than strolls casually, and always with a
definite destination rather than aimlessly. She does not linger, nor does
she pause to do a little window shopping. Instead, Jeunet's camera performs these functions, playing the role of *flâneur* as it drifts along the
streets and shopping arcades and into cafés and parks, evoking a Paris
that is more Baudelaire than Baedecker.

Baudelaire is considered to be the first great poet of the modern
city, and *Un Long dimanche de fiançailles* reflects these lyrical urban
rhythms, depicting 1920s Paris as a city teeming with life, where tradition (the farmers selling produce at the marketplace at Les Halles) rubs
shoulders with modernity (the architecturally monumental train stations,

Art Nouveau Métro entrance, Second Empire Opéra Garnier, and wide, Haussmannized boulevards buzzing with traffic noises). Tom Conley has written that "Baudelaire's city poetry was the first to translate the shock and pleasure of exile through an art of collage and scattering of images that betrays a movement of constant deterritorialization. Baudelaire's Paris conveys the experience of disaffected pleasure" (Conley 72). This "disaffected pleasure" both seduced and irritated some viewers of the film. For example, Sue Harris wrote in her review that "lush vistas and painterly compositions abound, delighting the eye, but deceiving the mind" (Harris, Review 78). *Un Long dimanche de fiançailles* presents a France taken from the pages of the tourist guides, but it does so from a perspective that is not simply promotional. Jeunet's camera sweeps through the covered arcades immortalized by Walter Benjamin at ground level, and we see only the massive iron legs of the Eiffel Tower when Elodie Gordes and her husband sit on a bench before it: we are at their level, not above them. The France that Jeunet presents is breathtakingly beautiful in the heritage cinema style, but it also questions this official version of French national identity, as Mathilde questions the official story of what happened to Manech.

Many of the Parisian locations depicted in the film ("depicted" rather than "shown," because most of these are digitally enhanced) are sites that a *flâneur* might well frequent: sites of leisure, shopping, and artistic consumption. We are shown the Place de l'Opéra, the covered shopping arcades, and Les Halles, whose stunning re-creation as a farmer's market cannot conceal its later incarnation as a shopping mall in the mind of any viewer with a passing familiarity with Paris. We also see the Gare d'Orsay, impressive because of its restoration and its inevitable association with the modern-day Musée d'Orsay on the same site, and a Métro station entrance in the ornate Art Nouveau style that came to symbolize Belle Époque France—both locations merging transportation with France's artistic *patrimoine,* suggesting the literal mobility of iconographic representations. Then there are the eating and drinking establishments: the opulent brasserie where Elodie Gordes and Biscotte go on a date, and the elegant café with the improbably well-appointed lavatory where Mathilde meets the German woman who has information about Manech; but also the working-class café-cum-bar on the rue de la Main d'or, with the one-armed bartender and the world-weary female patron of a certain age, which is more evocative of a poetic realist film than a tourist haunt. Finally, there is the ornate Pont Alexandre III, beneath which Tina Lombardi takes vengeance on one of the officials responsible for her lover's death: as we go under the bridge rather than gaze at it from above, we understand that we are seeing Paris from the ground up.

It is not only through the implicit association with Parisian locales that Baudelaire is invoked; lines from his poem "L'Albatros" are recited in the film. We first see the bird during an idyllic flashback to Mathilde and Manech's courtship in Brittany, after he has etched the initials "MMM" onto a church bell. As the lovers stand gazing at one of the birds circling gracefully in the sky, Manech tells Mathilde, "An albatross is stubborn. He knows he can outlast the wind." The bird next appears in another flashback (apparently predating the previous flashback), which takes place after Manech and Mathilde have made love for the first time and when Manech is carving the letters "MMM" onto a cliff face. There we again see the albatross (played with convincing naturalism by a gannet) flying majestically past the lovers. Later in the film, when Célestin Poux pays a visit to Sylvain and Bénédicte's home in Brittany in reponse to an ad placed by Mathilde, he recites a couple of lines from Baudelaire's poem: "[A]lbatros, vastes oiseaux des mers, / Qui suivent, indolents compagnons de voyage, / Le navire glissant sur les gouffres amers" (Albatrosses, vast seabirds, indolent traveling companions following the ship as it slips over bitter abysses). Poux is referring to the model of German warplane, also called an Albatross, from which a German soldier shot at Manech while he was (again) carving the initials "MMM" on a tree trunk.

Mathilde and Manech's liaison is thus associated on at least three occasions with Baudelaire—each allusion to an albatross building up to the climax of Poux's recitation of Baudelaire's poem. Manech and Mathilde, in their own ways, display traits that Baudelaire attributes to the seabird—a metaphor for the poet—whose majestic grace in the skies turns into awkwardness when imprisoned in the mundane world of lesser mortals. Manech is depicted as someone with his head in the clouds, whose youth and innocence are distinctly unsuited to the horrors of war. Mathilde is clearly the referent behind the bird's initial association with stubbornness, and the implication is that she too will "outlast the wind" of adversity. Like the regal birds trapped on a ship,

Mathilde is weighed down by her infirmity, her limp recalling the line from Baudelaire's poem about the birds dragging their wings, as they "[l]aissent piteusement leurs grandes ailes blanches / Comme des avirons traîner à côté d'eux" (pitifully let their great white wings drag beside them like oars), while one of the sailors "mime, en boitant, l'infirme qui volait!" (imitates, by limping, the once-flying cripple). Like the two opposing spheres of the poem (the celestial heights of poetic endeavor and the banal depths of quotidian existence), or the Manichean duality thematized in Baudelaire's poetry more generally (summed up in the title of his most famous collection, *Les Fleurs du mal* [Flowers of evil]), the albatross is a polyvalent symbol with two structurally opposed meanings, the seabird and the warplane, or bucolic idyll and state-of-the-art killing machine.

Similarly, in Jeunet's depiction of the battlefields of the Somme, where a large portion of the film is set, the trenches are presented as the flipside of modernity's drive for advancement, the primitive underbelly of social and industrial progress. The trenches provide basic, primitive living conditions, but at the same time they are the culmination of modernity. They are an in-between space, marking the frontier between German and French national identity as well as the border between civilization and barbarism. The trenches are a cliché in films about the First World War—in his DVD commentary, Jeunet emphasizes that in changing the snowy setting of Japrisot's novel to the overwhelming muddiness we see in the film, he was striving for an overtly clichéd depiction of the trenches. Trench warfare was an innovation of the First World War, which, along with the advent of mechanized weapons and transportation, increased the lethal capabilities of soldiers beyond those of hand-to-hand combat, allowing them to kill and maim from a distance. According to Tim Armstrong, "[T]he Great War was . . . a prosthetic war in the sense of attempting to radically extend human capabilities" (Armstrong 95). The methods that Tina Lombardi employs to murder those who played a role in condemning her lover to death mirror the war's more general deployment of killing by proxy. She kills Major Lavrouye, the official who used the stay of execution to repair his magnifying glass, by tying him to a bed and shooting at the mirror above him, causing its shards to impale him. The death of this character, played by Jean-Claude Dreyfus, replays in a more amplified form the death of the butcher (also played by

Dreyfus) in *Delicatessen* by a knife in the forehead, only in the later film, the weapon's trajectory is indirect, mediated by the mirror. Similarly, in the other scene in which Tina Lombardi kills an official (Thouvenel) who played a role in her lover's fate, she does so by pulling on her eyeglasses, which trigger a gun she wears on her waist. Both methods of murder allow Tina to remain literally outside the line of fire, like the soldiers in the trenches. However, as was the case for many of the soldiers who fought in the war (such as the German soldier who shoots at Manech from his warplane), this sanitized form of killing does not spare Tina herself from a grisly fate.

This roundabout way of engaging in, and with, violence is adopted by the film itself. Jeunet's film often veers slightly to one side of history instead of plowing right through it: but just as his stories and images threaten to divert our gaze from the trauma of war, they bring us back to it via a circuitous route. For example, in a film about the First World War whose plot revolves around self-mutilation, one would expect to see some dismemberment or prosthetic limbs. However, apart from the broken Christ hanging from a crucifix in the opening sequence, we are not shown any dismemberment, and we only see one artificial limb in the film, the wooden hand belonging to the owner of Louis's bar on, appropriately enough, the rue de la Main d'or (Street of the Golden Hand) (figure 30). When Mathilde asks Louis if he lost his hand in the war, he shakes his head and tells her that it was eaten by a hyena at the Jardin des Plantes. This anecdote is a reversal of the legend surrounding the Siege of Paris during the Franco-Prussian War, in which Parisians, suffering from severe food shortages, were said to have "eaten the zoo" at the Jardin des Plantes. Although Rebecca Spang has pointed out that it was actually the Jardin d'Acclimatation in the Bois de Boulogne that housed the animals that were eaten and that, contrary to popular belief, elephant and yak meat was not used to feed the impoverished but instead served as a delicacy for the monied classes, the legend of zoo animals at the Jardin des Plantes being eaten by the starving masses has been an enduring symbol of French suffering during the siege and the war—and by extension, war more generally. According to Spang, "The siege has been effectively totemized by a statement both horrified and bemused: 'They ate the zoo.' In anecdotal histories of diet or of menageries, as well as in academic studies of Paris, zoo-eating functions as a type of stigmata, as a sign of the suffering inflicted on the people of Paris by the besieging Prussians. Numbered among the war dead, the elephants and kangaroos even have their own memorial . . . [a]t the entrance to the Jardin des Plantes" (Spang 756). Louis's wooden hand, while at first appearing to deflect attention from the war, ends up bringing us right back to it: in many ways, the First World War functioned as an extension of the Franco-Prussian War, a kind of *revanche*, or revenge, for France's losses in the previous war. In this context, the anthropophagic hyena that feasted on Louis's hand would be exacting its own revenge for the apocryphal fate that befell its ancestors.

The main function of the hyena story, however, is as a pretext for the presence of Louis's prosthetic arm. It may seem perverse that, in a film about the First World War whose plot revolves around the mutilation and dismemberment of hands, the only prosthetic hand appears on a man whose injury did not result from the war. This prosthesis is in excess of the requirements of the narrative, a supplement like Mathilde's limp, which is not connected to the war. Mathilde's infirmity evokes the figure of the *mutilé de guerre* (war amputee) that haunted Europe for decades, serving as a constant reminder of the ravages of war, from actual limbless veterans to the ubiquitous signs in buses and the Métro instructing passengers to give up their seats to the wounded. The condition of Mathilde's leg is the subject of the film's last line of dialogue: when the lovers are reunited against the odds (though not against the expectations

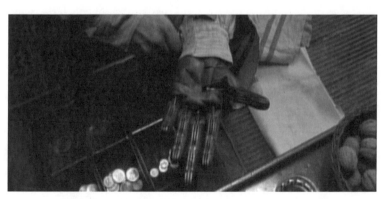

Figure 30. Wooden hand in *Un Long dimanche de fiançailles.*

set up by the film), Manech's first words to Mathilde are, "Does it hurt when you walk?" It is as though Mathilde, along with Germain Pire's young daughter, who also walks with a polio-inflicted limp, suffer from a sympathetic infirmity.

The hyena story, like Mathilde's limp, may exceed or skirt around the requirements of the narrative, but ultimately it is exactly suited to the symbolic requirements of the film. The hyena story at once deflects from and draws attention to the conflict between France and Germany. Similarly excessive to requirements of the narrative are the sumptuous locations and the painstaking re-creations of iconic sites of French national identity. In the way that the newsreels provide postcards of the past (whose authenticity is undermined by the use of obviously fictional footage), the highly stylized, idealized, and quintessentially French locations shown in the film provide postcards of a country whose cohesion is placed in question. The Parisian sites represent the official story of French history, in the same way that the War Ministry's account of Manech's fate is the official version of what happened. As the stock footage in *Un Long dimanche de fiançailles* functions as screen memories, images that divert attention from larger historically traumatic events, so the touristic sites depicted in the film deflect the gaze from the border zones of contested national identity.

The film's exploration of the themes of memory and history is thus a fitting addition to Jeunet's career, which has engaged with and emblematized the complexities of transnational cinema. The irony, for a film that thematizes prosthetic memory, is that Jeunet's film has now become a prosthetic memory of the First World War, standing in for personal memories of the war among members of the public too young to have lived through it themselves. This preoccupation with the ghosts of the past is ultimately bound to the film's transnational dimension. The transnational can be figured as a palimpsest or filmic dissolve suspended indefinitely at midpoint, with two or more countries at once visible and transparent. The transnational often (perhaps always) comprises a transhistorical dimension, as one country's history is invariably bound up in those of others: it is often the past that seeps through the filmy gauze of the present. In other words, the "there" is often inseparable from the "then" that comes to haunt the here and now. The transnational is a place that is not singular, not merely itself. It is the "other scene," as

Lacan might say; it is the unconscious of a place. *Un Long Dimanche de fiançailles,* with its persistent return to the past (each time revealing a different aspect of it, rewriting it a bit, remembering what has been dismembered), enacts this return to the site of the trauma, to the other scene—in this case, as in many, the theater of war. All of Jeunet's films in one way or another take us back to a different time and, at least by implication, a different place. This is what makes them such an integral part of the here and now.

Commentary by Jean-Pierre Jeunet |

This commentary, in which Jeunet spoke directly to the camera about his career and a variety of other subjects, was filmed for the television program *Auto/Focus*, which first aired in France on November 23, 2005, on France 4 (production KM; concept: Thinkfactory/Alexandre Drubigny; directed by Alexandre Drubigny). Translated from the French by Elizabeth Ezra.

(On *Once upon a Time in the West;* dir. Sergio Leone, 1969): I see myself at the age of seventeen in a cinema in Sable d'Olonne, and I'm sitting there, and it's killing me just watching a scene, seeing that camera movement. I realized then just how cinema can be magic, ludic—the marriage between the image and music. You know, I still have trouble talking about it. At the time, I was unable to speak for three days. I was the tormented adolescent, you see. My parents asked me, "What's the matter with you? Are you ill?" and I said, "You couldn't possibly understand." It was an enormous shock, a fantastic revelation. That's the magic of cinema.

(On *La nuit américaine* [Day for night]; dir. François Truffaut, 1973): This was one of the first films I saw in Nancy on my own in a cinema. When I saw this hymn to cinema, I knew that I had to do this. It couldn't be any other way; I knew I would do this. At the time, I had just started working for the telephone company. I had embarked on a career as a state worker which had nothing to do with cinema. But I knew, with an unshakable conviction, that I would make films.

Now, Truffaut is someone who fascinates me because he has a true love of cinema; in fact, for me he symbolizes the love of cinema. And yet I think he is—I'm going to say something awful here—I think he's quite a bad director. He's a very bad director of actors. I didn't make this up. I mean, it's obvious, but it's also something I've heard from lots of actors—he films very badly, and yet the awkwardness that he brings to his films gives them an added charm. And that's a very precious thing; he's very lucky. Perhaps not all his films; in the middle of the 1970s, he lost his touch a bit. But he's nonetheless someone who has an incredible charm. I miss him a lot. My great regret is to have missed my chance to speak to him when I won my first César award, for *Le Manège*, a short film. He was sitting on the steps, he was a little tired, it was the night he'd won all the Césars for *Le Dernier Métro*. I would have liked to go up to him and say, "Mr. Truffaut, I'm somewhat indebted to you for this César because of the influence *Day for Night* had on me." But I didn't have the nerve, I was an idiot, and today I regret it.

(On David Lynch): There's not a single film by David Lynch that I don't like. Even in the most difficult ones, like *Lost Highway*, there's always something that I find to be fantastic. He's enchanting. It's thanks to him that we found Angelo Badalamenti, the musician. He's someone I adore and whom I respect profoundly.

(On animation): Because I really liked animation, and because in the beginning I didn't have the means to make animated films, I started by writing about animation. With Caro and André Igual, we started up a journal called *Fantasmagorie*, and with Phil Casoar we wrote for *Charlie Mensuel* and *Fluide Glaciale,* and that got us invited to animation festivals all over the world—Zaghreb, Okawa, Annecy, of course—and to see all those films that we loved, and to travel. But I wasn't really a critic per se. Because we loved the films so much, instead of critiquing them, we tried to interview the animators and to promote them rather than criticize them.

I'm not sure I would still enjoy making animated films these days, because I think that I like the actors and the location scouting so much that I think I would have a hard time doing nothing but animation again. I just went to visit the Pixar studios last week, where [someone] asked me this very question. He said, "You see, everything's done on computer." And I thought, "No, these days, I really enjoy riding around on a scooter doing the location scouting in Paris, or doing the casting, discovering actors." The moment you discover an actor is such a magical moment. Animation is great, but it would deprive me of too many of those pleasures. I must confess that today, I can't stand films that aren't in 3D. I adore what Pixar does; I adore *Toy Story* and *Monsters, Inc.*, and that sort of thing, but I can't stand watching a traditional cartoon. I just can't do it anymore.

(On breaking into filmmaking): The important thing is just to make films. When kids ask me how to get into films, I always ask them if they want to make or to be—do they want to be a director, or do they want to make films? It's a question that seems strange to them and makes them think. It's true that what lots of wannabe directors really want is to walk on stage at the Cannes Film Festival, pick up girls, earn money, be in a magazine. But if they really want to do it, it's very simple. You get a camera, which is not very difficult today. It's not like in the old days, where you needed film stock and a laboratory, and it cost a lot of money. You get a camera, and you make a film—and stop going on about it. Obviously, this reply shocks them a bit, but that was always Caro's and my philosophy, and it has remained my philosophy: you get a camera, and you make a film. And if you make films, it's because you're happy making films. Subsequently, they might be successful, and if that's the case, then you progress from Super-8 to 16mm and then on to 35mm. Maybe you'll do it all in your kitchen with marionettes, or you might use actors, and maybe you'll find yourself one day making *Un Long dimanche de fiançailles* with two thousand people. But the main thing is just to make films. That's always been my philosophy.

When I made *Bunker de la dernière rafale* with Caro, we did everything ourselves. We didn't even have any equipment. . . . We had to do it all ourselves, the costumes, the sets, the storyboard. . . . We learned everything by doing. I think that the brain learns better when you do things yourself by trial and error than when you're taught a theory in a class by some professor who tells you to go off and do something.

(On the director Jean-Jacques Zilbermann): Jean-Jacques has been very supportive from the very beginning, because when we [rented out his cinema] to screen *Le Bunker de la dernière rafale*, which is a rather unusual film—it hits you over the head a bit—he laughed all the way through. It's not a comedy, but I found his laughter reassuring. It showed that there were people who were capable of appreciating the film's somewhat quirky humor. He became a great friend, and we offer moral support to one another during difficult times.

(On *Pas de repos pour Billy Brakko*): I must talk about the little stars you see in *Billy Brakko*. I drew them myself, directly on the surface of the film negative. I was in the developing laboratory, I asked to have the negative, and I scratched the stars onto the surface of the film. People were standing around me, because they had never seen anything like it. . . . This was a film that was made for thirty-five thousand francs. I simply had an overwhelming urge to do it: it was one of those times when you'd like to make a film but can't manage it, so you wait, you write feature films, you try to get funding, and no one wants to have anything to do with you. The first film I wrote with Caro was *La Cité des enfants perdus,* but clearly it would have been too expensive, and obviously it was too unusual, too bizarre. So at a certain point, I couldn't take it anymore, so I made *Billy Brakko* with thirty-five thousand francs. We were completetly incompetent; we didn't know how to do anything; we couldn't even load the camera. We had to reshoot several scenes because we messed them up. And then the film made a bit of a splash. It was the same for *Foutaises,* which was also a film I simply had an urge to make. I remember I made it with the money I owed on my taxes. I told them I couldn't pay; I asked for an extension of six months, and I used the money to make *Foutaises.* I then sold the film to Canal+ and used the money from the sale to pay my taxes. So, in fact, it was a film produced with money from French taxes, from the Ministry of Finance. Thank you, Ministry of Finance.

(On the producer Claudie Ossard): Claudie Ossard was the indispensable link for us. Wild, a bit punk, a connoisseur, and the best professional working in cinema. Without her, we would never have made a film. [Not long after we first met,] she told me that she only liked love stories. So when we had written the synopsis for *Delicatessen,* I remember we were at Cannes one day, and there was another producer—I don't remember who it was—and Claudie was standing nearby with a cinematographer. I started to talk about *Delicatessen* to the other producer, although in fact it was Claudie who interested me. She appeared to be listening in, so I said, "No, don't worry, you wouldn't like this. It's not a love story—you wouldn't be interested." And I continued to pitch *Delicatessen* to the other producer, while saying to Claudie, "This isn't for you, you wouldn't like it." Of course, the more I said this [the more interested she became].

(On the synchronized lovemaking sequence in *Delicatessen*): I remember very distinctly that when I talked about the idea for this sequence to Caro and Gilles Adrien, our cowriter, they both grimaced. It's a sequence that everyone wanted to cut. I fought to get it included in the film. I don't regret it, because . . . it became the symbol of *Delicatessen.* I think the idea came to me when I worked in a small animation studio at the very beginning of my career. [A colleague] lived in a place with a neighbor in the apartment above him who had a squeaky bed, and he would hear the couple above him, and he would come in to work and complain about the squeaking noise, and that's where I got the idea. Obviously, we worked with a metronome, because we would film one short scene one day, and the next day we'd shoot another, and then another scene after that, and we needed to know exactly where we were. That required a huge amount of preparation, with a storyboard, and a lot of precision.

(On the casting director Pierre-Jacques Bénichou): It's important to mention him because he's worked on all my films, apart from *Alien Resurrection,* which had an American casting director in place. But he's one of the loyal ones, and I really like to work with loyal people, that is, to be loyal to my technicians and to receive their loyalty in return. This osmosis, this artistic collaboration, is something precious because obviously, at a certain point, you know each other really well, and things go smoothly. I think Clint Eastwood works that way, always with the same team. Sure, in the beginning you make a few mistakes, there are a few mismatches, but after a few films you streamline, and you finally end up with a solid core of people. This core group I hope to take with me for the next film [*The Life of Pi*], which I hope to make in Hollywood. In any case, that's the arrangement I pitched to the first studio, Twentieth-Century Fox. They told me that they couldn't imagine it any other way. That must mean, then, that the collaborative spirit shines through the image, that you can see it and feel it, and that's something that's very precious to me.

(On Dominique Pinon): Dominique Pinon is my "fetish-actor." . . . It's not only because of his unusual face. It's above all because he's a very technical actor and because he does something different for each role, which is not the case with all actors. Without being unkind to anyone, lots of French actors are only capable of playing what they essentially are in real life, and they reproduce the same thing. Pinon is a rare actor, like those actors I so admired from after the war—Jouvet, Carette, Michel Simon, Saturnin Fabre—that whole family of actors. He's very inventive; he can play the devil in one film and something else in another. And on top of that, of course, there's that great face. . . .

(On Jean-Paul Belmondo): Belmondo is an actor from another cinema, from another life, another generation. He's an actor I could never see myself working with. He reminds me of the cinema of the 1970s, with . . . stories of lovers hiding in the closet—for me, it's like another planet. I have no disrespect for Mr. Belmondo, and I loved him in his early films, but from what he did afterwards and what he later became, I don't think our work will ever intersect. I'm not ashamed to say it; it's just that we seem to belong to different families.

(On *La Cité des enfants perdus*): The extreme technical complexity of this film meant that I had to shoot the absolute minimum of scenes necessary to make the film, because there was an immense set to light and enormous pressure with what's called a performance bond, which means that the insurance company is waiting in the wings, ready to replace you at any moment if anything goes wrong. So for many years, when I thought of *La Cité des enfants perdus,* I only considered its weak points, but more recently I've come to recognize its qualities, which are not lacking, and I find the corrosive attacks that were made on the film when it opened the Cannes festival to be unjustified. . . . I'm not interested in speaking about the critics, because I've personally never had any complaints, having been rather privileged in that regard. But it's true that the initial critical reaction to *La Cité* was awful. . . . A film is inscribed for all eternity on filmstock or now on DVD, but in fact, films don't exist as such. They only exist in their relation to the viewers watching them. There are as many films as there are viewers and as many films as there are subsequent re-viewings by individual spectators. As Jean-Jacques Zilbermann said, he saw *Cité* three times, and each time his perception of it was different. When critics or, indeed, ordinary viewers, declare that a film is bad, they should have the wisdom to see that if they watch it again in two years, they may well find it to be a good film, or at least they will see it in a different light.

(On *Alien Resurrection*): First of all, it was a huge personal adventure for the whole French team I took over with me. It affected our personal lives, because when you go abroad, everything's different and new, and because we were responsible for a budget of eighty million dollars, and because I didn't speak English—imagine trying to do everything with an interpreter who had to translate everything I said. I quickly established as an operating principle the fact that I would bring one of my own ideas to every scene; that way, I would feel that it was really my film. I think it was Kassovitz who gave me a very nice compliment in saying that this looks like a Jeunet film with aliens in it. I thought that was nice because it meant that I had found a way to make the film my own. When I returned to France after having spent some twenty months in Los Angeles, I remember that I was treated a bit like a French hero who has just won a gold medal at the Olympics. The critics (in France, at least) were ecstatic; in fact, in my opinion, they were too excessive in their praise. Even the one French critic who has lambasted all my other films liked *Alien Resurrection,* announcing that this was my best film. Which only goes to show that he knows nothing about cinema, because *Alien Resurrection* is only a sequel, and sequels by definition are devoid of interest, because the interest lies in creating an original film. People may wonder why I agreed to do the film, and the answer is that this was an extraordinary opportunity for a French director to make a big Hollywood film with all the resources of Hollywood at your disposal. Yet we still had quite a few difficulties, because in fact, many things didn't work very well, and Hollywood *savoir-faire* is sometimes a bit of a myth.

(On proposing ideas for *Alien Resurrection*): When I first arrived in Hollywood, because we had been beaten up a bit by the French critics over *La Cité des enfants perdus,* when the Americans said that they'd seen *Cité* five times and loved it, I initially thought they were being sarcastic, but then I realized that they weren't, because, after all, they had hired me to make *Alien Resurrection* on the basis of *Cité.* Not only because they saw in *Cité* a certain aesthetic (I had wanted, at first, to bring Caro with me to Hollywood for that reason, but ultimately he decided that he didn't want to make the film), but also because they saw the technical side of things, the special effects of *Cité,* as something that they wanted for *Alien.* They also liked the unusual ideas in the film, and they told me that, since they were already taking a big risk by making a new *Alien* film, they felt it would actually be less risky to take a risk with the kinds of ideas that I had. So, in fact, they welcomed all my ideas for the film and let me implement all of them, except for a handful that were too expensive—once again, a problem with money.

(On Sigourney Weaver): Sigourney, now there's a real personality, bigger than mine. She terrorizes everyone; everyone flees in terror from her. To be respected by her, you have to be strong. If you're not strong, she'll eat you alive. I remember that during a week early on in the shoot, I was really tired of it, she would constantly humiliate me in front of everyone. One day I snapped . . . and stormed off the set. I was sure I would be fired. Then I was summoned into her trailer, and she had a big smile on her face, all her anger had disappeared, and her good humor had returned. She's someone who requires a strong personality.

(On the controversy surrounding the national identity of *Un Long dimanche de fiançailles*): [Warner Brothers] tried to Americanize the film in the publicity campaign, but I don't think they were right to do so, because it caused a bit of confusion. Audiences in Japan and in the

United States were wondering whether it was an American film or a French film. I think they should have emphasized its Europeanness, but they didn't know how to do that, because it was the first time they had ever distributed a French film. That was the slight disadvantage of having the film distributed by a big American studio, but I was extremely proud to see the film with the Warner Brothers logo distributed across the globe. That's why I was very hurt by the whole polemic about whether this was a French film or not, which I know had nothing to do with me. It was purely a commercial issue, raised by people who didn't want to have to deal with competition. I was a bit disappointed by all the fuss. This film was an exceptional case; the rights to the book belonged to Warner Brothers in the United States, but it's a French book by Sébastien Japrisot. I was in talks with Warner, and I told them the project interested me, as long as I could jettison the script they had already come up with and rewrite it from scratch. They said that wouldn't be a problem. Then I told them I wanted to make the film entirely in French. They also said yes to that. And I demanded the final cut, which they also agreed to. This was unprecedented. We made a 100 percent French film, filmed in France, with a French crew, French technicians, but with American power behind it, because they distributed it around the world, and it had an enormous budget. Those were ideal conditions. I remember arriving on set with my director of photography, Bruno Delbonnel, looking up at the huge cranes and thinking we were in the middle of *War of the Worlds;* it was incredible. To think that we had made *Billy Brakko* for next to nothing. We looked at each other and said, "Hey, this isn't bad; maybe we'll get the chance to play with some of these toys." At the same time, there was complete and utter freedom.

However, having said that, I have great respect for the limitations of whatever budget I'm working with. I happen to have been born in 1953, so I'm from the postwar generation. My parents were from a rural background, where they had experienced not having enough to eat during the war, and they taught me to turn the light off when I leave a room. So I find the thought of going over budget very disturbing. I know a lot of directors who aren't bothered by going over budget and some who even make it a point of pride, but it would bother me, so I really try to respect the budget.

(On discovering Audrey Tautou): From the very start, she was a revelation. . . . The best moments of complicity that I've had with an actor have been with Audrey. I only regret that I don't know more about her life, because she is very secretive. But when it comes to work, I couldn't imagine having a better collaborative rapport with anyone.

(On the screenwriter Guillaume Laurant): Finding the right screenwriter is extremely important. In my collaboration with Guillaume Laurant, Guillaume essentially writes the dialogue. That's something that I don't know how to do, and I don't like doing it. When I hear dialogue I've written, it's sort of like hearing my own voice on the answering machine: I find it very unpleasant. It comes easily to Guillaume. As my films tend to have an atemporal quality and usually have a poetic, disconnected dimension, he has a knack for bringing in these unusual aspects, this flavor of Jacques Prévert, because, of course, Prévert has always been a major reference point. My meeting Laurant was a key moment in my career, and it was a question of fate, coincidence, chance. I adore stories about coincidences, as you can tell from *Amélie*. I adore Paul Auster, who also likes stories of this kind—I know that one day we'll work together. Perhaps it's not really a question of chance, though; life brings people together. Guillaume and I had to meet. Now I can't imagine working with anyone else on dialogue, because we think alike. When we watch television, sometimes we look at each other, and we don't even need to crack jokes anymore, because everything is communicated silently.

(On the painter Juarez Machado): You need visual references when you speak to your artistic collaborators, because it's easier to convey ideas by means of drawings or photos than it is through words, since words can be interpreted in so many ways. For *Amélie*, I'd found this artist's paintings to be absolutely perfect, especially the interaction between the colors, because it's more a question of the relationship among colors (obviously, the film doesn't resemble his paintings), and everyone had pictures of his paintings up on their walls—the costume designers, the set designers, the set decorators—and that guided us all in the same direction. Obviously, the director of photography had these paintings on his wall, too. Whenever I got the sense that things were straying a bit too far from the pictures, I would say, "Let's get back to those images," because they'd be covered with notes and bits of paper, and I'd say,

"Take all that other stuff down, and let's look at the pictures, let's take sustenance from them and use them as a guide." We do that for every film. In fact, it was Caro who first used Machado's reds and greens, on *La Cité des enfants perdus*. It always irritates me a little when I hear people say that *Amélie* is full of reds and greens, when in fact *Amélie* is yellow and gold; it's the publicity poster that's red and green. Now, *Cité* is a red and green film, and that was Caro's idea, because of the film's allusions to Christmas and Santa Claus.

(On his working habits): I don't really blow up during a shoot; however, sometimes the assistants blow up because I don't praise them enough. They say, "You know, sometimes it would be nice if you'd throw us a bone; we're not that different from dogs in that respect." They're right: I'm not good at giving compliments. What I tend to do is crack the whip. I remember that while I was filming *Alien Resurrection*, there was graffiti in the bathroom that read "Jean-Pierre Jeunet, non merci" [no thank you/no mercy]. I have a bit of a tendency to be like that. I'm hard on others because I'm hard on myself. If I'm a workhorse, it's because I love the work, not because I have to force myself. I can go the long haul. It's funny: it was Truffaut who said, "When you're making a film, you get the feeling that you're invincible, that nothing can touch you." I had that feeling when I was making *Dimanche*, which was a very physical film to make, with a very long, six-month shoot. I didn't get so much as a cold, while everyone around me was being struck down one by one with various ailments. And the minute the film was finished, my body seemed to collapse. But while you're filming, you're carried along by the dynamic; you're dragged along like a train pushing on in the night, as Truffaut used to say.

(On the success of *Amélie*): The year *Amélie* came out was an incredible year for us, full of amazing surprises. Not a day went by without some more good news. [One of the producers] and I would call each other and say, "Have you seen the paper?" . . . It never stopped. And the phenomenon was quite exceptional, because here was a *film d'auteur*, a quirky film, with twenty minutes of exposition and introduction in voiceover—in fact, I once saw a television program in which it was said that the techniques we used in *Amélie* were precisely what you're not supposed to do when you make a film—and yet, according to the same program, these techniques somehow work in *Amélie*. That's why I was nervous when it opened. I was thinking, "This will never work, with its twenty minutes of exposition, and so on." In spite of everything, it was first a critical success and then a worldwide popular success, and it also received acclaim from within the profession—I think it won about fifty prizes and was nominated for five Oscars. It was a filmmaker's dream: you write your little personal film, and then it becomes massive. It's what every filmmaker hopes for. But the phenomenal response from the public was a miracle, and I'm very lucky to have experienced it.

(On filmmaking): You don't make films for the public; you make them for yourself. You make them for your own satisfaction. You make the film that you want to go see but which doesn't exist until you make it. If you make it with real sincerity, and if you make the best thing you can make, then there's a chance it will be well received by the public. I often make the following comparison: Making films is a little bit like cooking. You prepare a dish, adding a pinch of this and a splash of that, and tasting it once in a while to see if it needs anything. When it's finished, you want to share it with the public, inviting them to taste it. You say, "Here, what do you think? How do you like it? Pretty good, huh?" That's my conception of cinema: a kind of cooking you do because you like to do it but that you then try to share with others.

Feature Films

Delicatessen (1991)
France
Production: CNC, StudioCanal, Constellation, U.G.C.–Hachette Première,
    Sofinergie, Sofinergie 2, Investimage 2, Investimage 3, Fondation Gan
Producer: Claudie Ossard
Directors: Marc Caro, Jean-Pierre Jeunet
Screenplay: Gilles Adrien, Marc Caro, Jean-Pierre Jeunet
Cinematography: Darius Khondji
Editor: Hervé Schneid
Music: Carlos D'Alessio
Sound: Jérôme Thiault
Production Designer: Marc Caro
Art Director: Jean Rabasse
Set Decorator: Aline Bonetto
Costume Designer: Valérie Pozzo di Borgo
Special Effects: Jean-Baptiste Bonetto, Yves Domenjoud, Olivier Gleyze
Visual Effects: Baptiste Magnien, Pitof, Antoine Simkine
Cast: Pascal Benezech (Tried to escape), Dominique Pinon (Louison), Marie-
    Laure Dougnac (Julie Clapet), Jean-Claude Dreyfus (Butcher), Karin
    Viard (Mademoiselle Plusse), Ticky Holgado (Monsieur Tapioca), Anne-
    Marie Pisani (Madame Tapioca), Boban Janevski (Tapioca boy), Mikael
    Todde (Tapioca boy), Edith Ker (Grandmother Tapioca), Rufus (Robert
    Kube), Jacques Mathou (Roger), Howard Vernon (Frog Man), Chick
    Ortega (Postman), Silvie Laguna (Aurore Interligator), Perrier Dominique
    Zardi (Taxi driver), Patrick Paroux (Puk), Maurice Lamy (Pank), Marc Caro
    (Fox), Eric Averloant (Tourneur), Dominique Bettenfeld (Troglodiste),
    Jean-Luc Caron (Troglodiste), Bernard Flavien (Troglodiste), David
    Defever (Troglodiste), Raymond Forestier (Troglodiste), Robert Baud
    (Troglodiste), Clara (Livingstone)
Color
99 min.

La Cité des enfants perdus (The city of lost children; 1995)
France/Germany/Spain
Production: Lumière, Studiocanal France, France 3 Cinéma, Elias Querejeta
   PC SL, Tele München, CNC
Producer: Claudie Ossard
Directors: Jean-Pierre Jeunet and Marc Caro
Screenplay: Gilles Adrien, Jean-Pierre Jeunet, Marc Caro, Guillaume Laurant
Cinematography: Darius Khondji, Michel Amathieu
Editor: Hervé Schneid
Music: Angelo Badalamenti
Production Designers: Marc Caro, Jean Rabasse
Art Director: Jean Rabasse
Set Decorators: Aline Bonetto, Georges Mougine, Denis Ozenne
Costume Designer: Jean-Paul Gaultier
Special Effects: Philippe Alleton, Jean-Baptiste Bonetto, Yves Domenjoud,
   Jean-Christophe Spadaccini
Visual Effects: Pitof, Antoine Simkine, Sebastien Caudron
Cast: Ron Perlman (One), Daniel Emilfork (Krank), Judith Vittet (Miette),
   Dominique Pinon (Diver/Clones), Jean-Claude Dreyfus (Marcello),
   Geneviève Brunet (Octopus sister), Odile Mallet (Octopus sister), Mireille
   Mossé (Mademoiselle Bismuth), Serge Merlin (Cyclops leader), Rufus
   (Peeler), Ticky Holgado (Circus barker), Joseph Lucien (Denrée), Mapi
   Galán (Woman in bar), Briac Barthelemy (Bottle), Pierre-Quentin Faesch
   (Pipo), Alexis Pivot (Tadpole), Léo Rubion (Jeannot), Guillaume Billod-
   Morel (Child), François Hadji-Lazaro (Killer), Dominique Bettenfeld
   (Bogdan), Lotfi (Melchior), Thierry Gibault (Brutus), Marc Caro (Brother
   Ange-Joseph), Jean-Louis Trintignant (Irvin the Brain), Ham-Chau Luong
   (Tattoo artist), Bezak (Helmsman), Hong Maï Thomas (Tattoo artist's
   wife), Frankie (Barmaid), René Pivot (Glazier), Daniel Adric (Cyclops),
   Christophe Salengro (Soldier), René Marquant (Captain), Enrique
   Villanueva (Spaniard), Dominique (Tied-up guard), Nane Germon (Miette,
   age 82), Mathieu Kassovitz (Man in crowd)
Color
112 min.

Alien Resurrection (1997)
USA
Production: Twentieth-Century Fox, Brandywine
Producers: Bill Badalato, Gordon Carroll, David Giler, Walter Hill, Sigourney
   Weaver
Director: Jean-Pierre Jeunet
Screenplay: Joss Whedon (based on characters by Dan O'Bannon and Ronald
   Shusett)

Cinematography: Darius Khondji
Editor: Hervé Schneid
Music: John Frizzell
Production Designer: Nigel Phelps
Art Director: Andrew Neskoromny
Set Decorator: John M. Dwyer
Costume Designer: Bob Ringwood
Visual Effects Supervisors: Pitof, Erik Henry
Cast: Sigourney Weaver (Ellen Ripley), Winona Ryder (Annalee Call),
    Dominique Pinon (Vriess), Ron Perlman (Johner), Gary Dourdan
    (Christie), Michael Wincott (Frank Elgyn), Kim Flowers (Sabra Hillard),
    Dan Hedaya (Gen. Martin Perez), J. E. Freeman (Dr. Mason Wren), Brad
    Dourif (Dr. Jonathan Gediman), Raymon Cruz (Vincent Distephano),
    Leland Orser (Larry Purvis), Carolyn Campbell (Anesthesiologist), Marlene
    Bush (Scientist), David St. James (Surgeon), Rodney Mitchell (Soldier with
    glove), Robert Faltisco (Soldier shot through helmet), David Rowe (Frozen
    soldier), Nicole Fellows (Young Ripley), Tom Woodruff Jr. (Lead alien)
Color
109 min./116 min. (2003 Special Edition)

Le Fabuleux Destin d'Amélie Poulain (Amélie; 2001)
France/Germany
Production: UGC Images, Victoire Productions, Tapioca Films, France 3
    Cinéma, MMC Independent GMBH, Sofinergie 5, Filmstiftung, Canal+
Producer: Claudie Ossard
Director: Jean-Pierre Jeunet
Screenplay: Guillaume Laurant, Jean-Pierre Jeunet
Cinematography: Bruno Delbonnel
Sound: Jean Umansky
Editor: Hervé Schneid
Music: Yann Tiersen
Set Designer: Aline Bonetto
Costume Designer: Madeline Fontaine
Cast: Audrey Tautou (Amélie Poulain), Mathieu Kassovitz (Nino
    Quincampoix), Rufus (Raphaël Poulain), Lorella Cravotta (Amandine
    Poulain), Serge Merlin (Raymond Dufayel), Jamel Debbouze (Lucien),
    Clotilde Mollet (Gina), Claire Maurier (Suzanne), Isabelle Nanty
    (Georgette), Dominique Pinon (Joseph), Artus de Penguern (Hipolito),
    Yolande Moreau (Madeleine Wallace), Urbain Cancelier (Collignon),
    Maurice Bénichou (Dominique Bretodeau), Michel Robin (Mr. Collignon),
    Andrée Damant (Mrs. Collignon), Claude Perron (Eva), Armelle
    (Philomène), Ticky Holgado (Man in photo who describes Amélie to
    Nino), Kevin Fernandes (Bretodeau as a child), Flora Guiet (Amélie, age

6), Amaury Babault (Nino as a child), André Dussolier (Narrator), Frédéric Mitterrand (Himself, voice)
Color/Black and white
129 min. (France); 122 min. (elsewhere)

Un Long dimanche de fiançailles (A very long engagement; 2004)
France/USA
Production: 2003 Productions, Warner Brothers France, Tapioca Films, TF1 Films Production, Canal+
Producers: Bill Gerber, Jean-Marc Deschamps, Jean-Lou Monthieux, Jean-Pierre Jeunet, Francis Boespflug
Director: Jean-Pierre Jeunet
Screenplay: Jean-Pierre Jeunet, Guillaume Laurant, based on the novel by Sébastien Japrisot
Cinematography: Bruno Delbonnel
Music: Angelo Badalamenti
Editor: Hervé Schneid
Set Designer: Aline Bonetto
Costume Designer: Madeline Fontaine
Cast: Audrey Tautou (Mathilde), Gaspard Ulliel (Manech), Dominique Pinon (Sylvain), Chantal Neuwirth (Bénédicte), André Dussollier (Pierre-Marie Rouvières), Ticky Holgado (Germain Pire), Marion Cotillard (Tina Lombardi), Dominique Bettenfeld (Ange Bassignano), Jodie Foster (Elodie Gordes), Jean-Pierre Darroussin (Benjamin Gordes), Clovis Cornillac (Benoît Notre-Dame), Jean-Pierre Becker (Lieutenant Esperanza), Denis Lavant (Six-Sous), Jérôme Kircher (Bastoche), Albert Dupontel (Célestin Poux), Jean-Paul Rouve (Postman), Elina Löwensohn (German woman), Julie Depardieu (Véronique Passavant), Michel Vuillermoz (L'il Louis), Urbain Cancelier (Priest), Maud Rayer (Mme. Desrochelles), Michel Robin (Old Man visiting battlefield), Tchéky Karyo (Captain Favourier), Jean-Claude Dreyfus (Commandant Lavrouye), Philippe Duquesne (Favart), Bouli Lanners (Chardolot), Stéphane Butet (Philippot), Christian Pereira (Archives officer), François Levantal (Thouvenel), Solène Le Pechon (Mathilde, age 10), Virgil Leclaire (Manech, age 13), Florence Thomassin (Narrator, voice), Thierry Gibault (Lieutenant Estrangin), Myriam Roustan (Café prostitute), Gilles Masson (Murdered officer), Sandrine Rigaud (Mariette Notre-Dame), Michel Chalmeau (Priest of Milly), Marc Faure (Prison director), Rodolphe Pauly (Jean Desrochelles), Xavier Maly (Chardolot's friend), Till Bahlmann (German prisoner), Tony Gaultier (Gravedigger), Louis-Marie Audubert (Gravedigger), Jean-Gilles Barbier (Sergeant)
Color
133 min.

Short Films

L'évasion (The escape; 1978)
Animation (marionettes)
France
Directors: Jean-Pierre Jeunet, Marc Caro
Color
7 min.

Le Manège (The carousel; 1979)
Animation (marionettes)
France
Production: Cinémation
Director: Jean-Pierre Jeunet
Screenplay: Jean-Pierre Jeunet
Camera: Jean-Pierre Jeunet
Sound: Bruno Delbonnel
Editors: Manuel Otero, Jean-Pierre Jeunet
Music: Philippe Sarde
Marionettes (design and manipulation): Marc Caro
Color
10 min.

Le Bunker de la dernière rafale (The bunker of the last gunshots; 1981)
France
Production: Zootrope
Directors: Marc Caro and Jean-Pierre Jeunet
Screenplay: Gilles Adrien, Marc Caro, Jean-Pierre Jeunet
Cinematography: Marc Caro, Jean-Pierre Jeunet, Spot
Editors: Marc Caro and Jean-Pierre Jeunet
Cast: Jean-Marie de Busscher, Marc Caro, Patrice Succi, Gilles Adrien, Spot,
    Vincent Ferniot, Thierry Fournier, Zorin, Eric Caro, Jean-Pierre Jeunet,
    Bruno Richard, Hervé di Rosa
Black and white/Color
26 min.

Pas de repos pour Billy Brakko (No rest for Billy Brakko; 1984)
France
Director: Jean-Pierre Jeunet
Screenplay: Jean-Pierre Jeunet
Editor: Jean-Pierre Jeunet
Photography: Bruno Delbonnel

Cast: Jean Bouise (Narrator, voice), Marc Caro, Phil Gascar, Jean-Pierre
Jeunet, Spot
Color
4½ min.

Foutaises (Trifles; 1989)
France
Director: Jean-Pierre Jeunet
Screenplay: Bruno Delbonnel, Jean-Pierre Jeunet
Cinematography: Jean Poisson
Music: Carlos D'Alessio
Costume Designer: Valérie Pozzo di Borgo
Cast: Dominique Pinon, Chick Ortega, Marie-Laure Dougnac, Diane
Bertrand, Fabienne Chaudat, Cindy, Delphine Colin, Céline Dubois,
Mathieu Duvanel, Maurice Lamy, Macalou, Philippe Miot, Philippe
Paimblanc, Daniel Poupry, Jean-Pierre Rata, Sébastien Seveau, Gérald
Weingand
Black and white
8 min.

Abraham, Nicolas, and Maria Torok. *The Shell and the Kernel: Renewals of Psychoanalysis.* Ed. and trans. Nicholas T. Rand. Chicago: University of Chicago Press, 1994.

Affron, Charles, and Mirella Jona Affron. *Sets in Motion: Art Direction and Film Narrative.* New Brunswick, N.J.: Rutgers University Press, 1995.

Andrew, Dudley. "*Amélie,* or *Le Fabuleux Destin du Cinéma Français.*" *Film Quarterly* 57.3 (2004): 34–46.

———. *Mists of Regret: Culture and Sensibility in Classic French Film.* Princeton, N.J.: Princeton University Press, 1995.

Andrew, Dudley, and Steven Ungar. *Popular Front Paris and the Poetics of Culture.* Cambridge, Mass.: Harvard University Press, 2005.

Armstrong, Tim. *Modernism, Technology, and the Body: A Cultural Study.* Cambridge: Cambridge University Press, 1998.

Augé, Marc. *Non-Places: Introduction to an Anthropology of Supermodernity.* London: Verso, 1995.

Barnier, Martin. "Amélie révise son histoire." *Vingtième Siècle* 74.2 (2002): 163–65.

Battaglia, Debbora. "Multiplicities: An Anthropologist's Thoughts on Replicants and Clones in Popular Film." *Critical Inquiry* 27 (Spring 2001): 493–514.

Baudrillard, Jean. *The Transparency of Evil.* Trans. James Benedict. London: Verso, 1993.

Bayon. "*Alien, la résurrection.*" *Libération,* November 12, 1997.

Bazin, André. *What Is Cinema?* Trans. Hugh Gray. Berkeley: University of California Press, 1967.

Benjamin, Walter. "The Work of Art in the Age of Mechanical Reproduction." In *Illuminations.* Ed. Hannah Arendt. Trans. Harry Zohn. New York: Schocken Books, 1969. 217–51.

Bergson, Henri. "Laughter." In *Comedy.* Ed. Wylie Sypher. Trans. Fred Rothwell. Garden City, N.Y.: Doubleday, 1956. 61–190.

Bergstrom, Janet. "Emigrés or Exiles? The French Directors' Return from Hollywood." In *Hollywood and Europe: Economics, Culture, National Identity,*

1945–95. Ed. Geoffrey Nowell-Smith and Stephen Ricci. London: British Film Institute, 1998. 86–103.

Braidotti, Rosi. *Metamorphoses: Towards a Materialist Theory of Becoming.* Cambridge: Polity Press, 2002.

Bruyn, Olivier de. "*Alien, la résurrection.*" *L'évènement,* November 13, 1997.

Bukatman, Scott. *Terminal Identity: The Virtual Subject in Post-Modern Science Fiction.* Durham, N.C.: Duke University Press, 1993.

Campion, A. "Jean-Pierre Jeunet ressuscite les 'aliens.'" *Journal du dimanche,* November 9, 1997.

Caruth, Cathy. "Unclaimed Experience: Trauma and the Possibility of History." *Yale French Studies* 79 (1991): 181–92.

Clover, Carol. "Her Body, Himself: Gender in the Slasher Film." *Representations* 20 (Fall 1987): 187–228.

Conley, Tom. "Paris as Map in Film, 1924–34." In *Parisian Fields.* Ed. Michael Sheringham. London: Reaktion, 1996. 71–84.

Constable, Catherine. "Becoming the Monster's Mother: Morphologies of Identity in the *Alien* Series." In *Alien Zone II.* Ed. Annette Kuhn. London: Verso, 1999. 173–202.

Copperman, Annie. "Vive la France!" *Les Echoes,* November 17, 1997.

Creed, Barbara. *The Monstrous-Feminine: Film, Feminism, Psychoanalysis.* London: Routledge, 1993.

Cubitt, Sean. "Delicatessen: Eco-Apocalypse in the New French Science Fiction Cinema." In *Aliens R Us: The Other in Science Fiction Cinema.* Ed. Ziauddin Sardar and Sean Cubitt. London: Pluto Press, 2002. 18–33.

Cuyer, Clément. "'Un long dimanche de fiançailles' n'est plus français!" *Allocine.* November 26, 2004. July 18, 2006. http://www.allocine.fr/article/fichearticle_gen_carticle=18367724.html.

Debemardi, Franck. "Entretien avec Marc Caro." *Faille Temporelle* 10. [Undated.] March 14, 2006. http://temporalistes.free.fr/FailleTemporelle/FT10/Caro/Caro.html.

Derrida, Jacques. *Mal d'Archive.* Paris: Galilée, 1995.

———. *Of Grammatology.* Trans. Gayatri Chakravorty Spivak. Baltimore: Johns Hopkins University Press, 1976.

Doane, Mary Ann. *The Emergence of Cinematic Time.* Cambridge, Mass.: Harvard University Press, 2002.

Donadey, Anne. "'Une Certaine Idée de la France: The Algeria Syndrome and Struggles over 'French' National Identity." In *Identity Papers: Contested Nationhood in Twentieth-Century France.* Ed. Steven Ungar and Tom Conley. Minneapolis: University of Minnesota Press, 1996. 215–32.

Drubigny, Alexandre, dir. *Auto/Focus.* Interviews with Jean-Pierre Jeunet. France 4 television. Prod. KM. First aired November 23, 2005.

Dufreigne, Jean-Pierre. "Alien se fait deux copines." *L'Express,* November 13, 1997.

Eaton, Michael. "Born Again." *Sight and Sound* 7.12 (December 1997): 6–9.

Ezra, Elizabeth. "Apocalypse Then: French Disaster Films of the 1920s." *Studies in French Cinema* 1.1 (2001): 5–12.

———. "Becoming Women: Cinema, Gender, and Technology." In *A 'Belle Epoque'? Women in French Society and Culture, 1890–1914.* Ed. Diana Holmes and Carrie Tarr. New York: Berghahn Books, 2006. 125–36.

———. *Georges Méliès: The Birth of the Auteur.* Manchester: Manchester University Press, 2000.

Fédida, Pierre. "Destins du cannibalisme." *Nouvelle Revue de Psychanalyse* 6 (Fall 1972): 123–27.

"Film Ruled 'Not French Enough.'" *BBC News*, November 27, 2004. July 18, 2006. http://news.bbc.co.uk/1/hi/entertainment/film/4048439.stm.

Finkielkraut, Alain. *La Mémoire vaine.* Paris: Gallimard, 1989.

Frazer, John. *Artificially Arranged Scenes.* Boston: G. K. Hall and Co., 1979.

Freud, Sigmund. "The 'Uncanny.'" In *Collected Papers.* Vol. 4. Trans. Joan Riviere. 1919; reprint, New York: Basic Books, 1959. 368–407.

Garber, Marjorie. *Vested Interests.* London: Penguin Books, 1993.

Gilroy, Paul. *Between Camps: Race, Identity, and Nationalism at the End of the Colour Line.* London: Allen Lane/Penguin Press, 2000.

Girard, René. *The Violence and the Sacred.* Baltimore: Johns Hopkins University Press, 1979.

Greenberg, Harvey R., M.D. "Reimagining the Gargoyle: Psychoanalytic Notes on *Alien.*" In *Close Encounters: Film, Feminism and Science Fiction.* Ed. Constance Penley, Elisabeth Lyon, Lynn Spigel, and Janet Bergstrom. Minneapolis: University of Minnesota Press, 1991. 83–104.

Greene, Naomi. *Landscapes of Loss: The National Past in Postwar French Cinema.* Princeton, N.J.: Princeton University Press, 1999.

Harris, Sue. "The Cinéma du Look." In *European Cinema.* Ed. Elizabeth Ezra. Oxford: Oxford University Press, 2004. 219–32.

———. Review of *A Very Long Engagement. Sight and Sound* 15.2 (February 2005): 76–78.

Hayes, Graeme. "Replaying History as Farce: Postmodernism and the Construction of Vichy in *Delicatessen.*" *Modern and Contemporary France* 7.2 (May 1999): 197–208.

Hayes, Graeme, and Martin O'Shaugnessy. "French Cinema: Globalization, Representation, and Resistance." *French Politics, Culture, and Society* 23.3 (Winter 2005): 1–13.

Hayward, Susan. "Cocteau's Belle Is Not That Bête: Jean Cocteau's *La Belle et la Bête.*" In *French Film: Texts and Contexts.* Ed. Susan Hayward and Ginette Vincendeau. London: Routledge, 1990. 127–36.

Horkheimer, Max, and Theodor Adorno. *The Dialectic of Enlightenment* Trans. John Cumming. 1944; reprint, New York: Continuum, 1990.

Howe, Desson. "*Alien Resurrection:* She Lives." *Washington Post,* November 28, 1997.

Hunt, Lynn. *The Family Romance of the French Revolution.* Los Angeles: University of California Press, 1992.

Hunter, Stephen. "*Alien Resurrection:* Birth of the Ooze." *Washington Post,* November 26, 1997.

James, Christine. "Alien Resurrection." *Boxoffice.* 1997. July 19, 2006. http://www.boxoffice.com/scripts/fiw.dll?GetReview&where=Name&terms=ALI EN+RESURRECTIO.

Jameson, Fredric. *Signatures of the Visible.* London: Routledge, 1990.

Japrisot, Sébastien. *Un Long dimanche de fiançailles.* 1991; reprint, Paris: Gallimard Folio, 2004.

Jeunet, Jean-Pierre, dir. *Alien Resurrection.* Special Edition DVD. Twentieth-Century Fox Home Entertainment, 2004.

———, and Marc Caro, dirs. *La Cité des enfants perdus.* DVD. Studio Canal, 2003.

———, and Marc Caro, dirs. *Delicatessen.* DVD. Studio Canal, 2003.

Kaes, Anton. "The Cold Gaze: Notes on Mobilization and Modernity." *New German Critique* 59 (Spring/Summer 1993): 105–17.

Kaganski, Serge. "Amélie pas jolie." *Libération,* May 31, 2001.

Kempley, Rita. "*Delicatessen.*" *Washington Post,* April 17, 1992. July 18, 2006. www.washingtonpost.com/wp-srv/style/longterm/movies/videos/delicatessenrkempley_a0a2b5.htm.

Kracauer, Sigfried. *From Caligari to Hitler: A Psychological History of the German Film.* Ed. and intro. Leonardo Quaresima. 1947; reprint, Princeton, N.J.: Princeton University Press, 2004.

Kristeva, Julia. *Pouvoirs de l'horreur.* Paris: Editions du Seuil, 1980.

———. *Strangers to Ourselves.* Trans. Leon S. Roudiez. New York: Columbia University Press, 1991.

Lançon, Phillipe. "Le frauduleux destin d'Amélie Poulain." *Libération,* June 1, 2001.

Landsberg, Alison. *Prosthetic Memory.* New York: Columbia University Press, 2004.

Lebrun, Dominique. *Paris-Hollywood.* N.p.: Fernand Hazen, 1987.

Lipovetsky, Gilles. *L'ère du vide.* Paris: Gallimard, 1993.

Méliès, Gaston. *Le Voyage autour du monde de la G. Méliès Manufacturing Company.* Paris: Association Les Amis de Georges Méliès, 1988.

Meusy, Jean-Jacques. *Paris-Palaces, ou le temps des cinemas (1894–1918).* Paris: CNRS Editions, 1995.

Miller, Laura. "Return of the Vagina Dentata from Outer Space!" *Salon,* November 26, 1997. July 18, 2006. http://www.salon.com/ent/movies/1997/11/26alien.html.

Mulvey, Laura. "Visual Pleasure and Narrative Cinema." *Screen* 16.3 (Autumn 1975): 6–18.

Nora, Pierre. "Between Memory and History: *Les Lieux de Mémoire*." *Representations* 26 (Spring 1989): 7–25.

Penley, Constance. *The Future of an Illusion: Film, Feminism, and Psychoanalysis*. London: Routledge, 1989.

Perec, Georges. "J'aime, je n'aime pas." *L'Arc* 76 (1979): 38–39.

Powrie, Phil. "The Fabulous Destiny of the Accordion in French Cinema." In *Changing Tunes: The Use of Pre-existing Music in Film*. Ed. Phil Powrie and Robynn Stilwell. Aldershot, U.K.: Ashgate, 2006. 137–51.

———. *Jean-Jacques Beineix*. Manchester: Manchester University Press, 2001.

Rony, Fatimah Tobing. *The Third Eye: Race, Cinema, and Ethnographic Spectacle*. Durham, N.C.: Duke University Press, 1996.

Rosello, Mireille. "Auto-portraits glanés et plaisirs partagés: *Les glaneurs et la glaneuse* et *Le fabuleux destin d'Amélie Poulain*." In *Les Fabuleuses Glaneuses du Cinéma Français Contemporain*. Special issue of *Esprit créateur* 42.2 (Fall 2002): 3–16.

———. *Postcolonial Hospitality: The Immigrant as Guest*. Stanford, Calif.: Stanford University Press, 2001.

Rosen, Philip. *Change Mummified*. Minneapolis: University of Minnesota Press, 2001.

Ross, Kristin. *Fast Cars, Clean Bodies*. Cambridge: Massachusetts Institute of Technology Press, 1995.

Rousso, Henry. *Le Syndrome de Vichy*. Paris: Seuil, 1990.

Rouyer, Philippe, and Yann Tobin. "Entretien Jean-Pierre Jeunet." *Positif* 443 (January 1998): 95–99.

Scatton-Tessier, Michelle. "Le Petisme: Flirting with the Sordid in *Le Fabuleux Destin d'Amélie Poulain*." *Studies in French Cinema* 4.3 (2004): 197–207.

Schlockoff, Alain, and Cathy Karani. "Excerpts from a Conversation with Jean-Pierre Jeunet and Marco Caro." 1995. July 18, 2006. http://www.sonypictures.com/classics/city/misc/interview.html#Q2.

Schwartz, Hillel. *The Culture of the Copy: Striking Likenesses, Unreasonable Facsimiles*. New York: Zone Books, 1996.

Showalter, Elaine. *Sexual Anarchy*. London: Bloomsbury, 1991.

Singh, Simon. *The Code Book*. London: Fourth Estate, 1999.

Spang, Rebecca. "And They Ate the Zoo: Relating Gastronomic Exoticism in the Siege of Paris." *Modern Language Notes* 107.4 (1992): 752–73.

Stacey, Jackie. "She Is Not Herself: The Deviant Relations of *Alien Resurrection*." *Screen* 44.3 (Autumn 2003): 251–76.

Stack, Peter. "*Alien* All Guts, No Glory." *San Francisco Chronicle*, November 26, 1997.

Tatara, Paul. Review of *Alien Resurrection*. *CNN Interactive*, November 20, 1997. July 18, 2006. http://edition.cnn.com/SHOWBIZ/9711/20/review.alien/index.html.

Telotte, J. P. "The Doubles of Fantasy and the Space of Desire." In *Alien Zone*. Ed. Annette Kuhn. London: Verso, 1990. 152–59.

Thomson, David. *The Alien Quartet*. London: Bloomsbury, 1998.

Tirard, Laurent. "Master Class with Jean-Pierre Jeunet." *Moviemakers' Master Class*. New York: Faber and Faber, 2002. 111–22.

Tobias, Scott. "Interview with Jean-Pierre Jeunet." *The Onion*, October 31, 2001. July 5, 2006. http://www.avclub.com/content/node/22708.

Turan, Kenneth. "She's Alive! It's Alive!" *Los Angeles Times*, November 26, 1997.

Vincendeau, Ginette. "Café Society." *Sight and Sound* 11.8 (August 2001): 22–25.

———. "Fathers and Daughters in French Cinema: From the 20s to 'La Belle Noiseuse.'" In *Women and Film: A* Sight and Sound *Reader*. Ed. Pam Cook and Philip Dodd. Philadelphia: Temple University Press, 1993. 156–63.

———. "Miss France." *Sight and Sound* 15.2 (February 2005): 13–15.

———, ed. *Film/Literature/Heritage*. London: British Film Institute, 2001.

Virilio, Paul. *War and Cinema*. Trans. Patrick Camiller. London: Verso, 1989.

White, Hayden. "The Modernist Event." In *The Persistence of History*. Ed. Vivian Sobchack. New York: Routledge, 1996. 17–38.

Williams, Linda. "When the Woman Looks." In *Film Theory and Criticism*. 4th ed. Ed. Gerald Mast, Marshall Cohen, and Leo Brandy. New York: Oxford University Press, 1992. 561–77.

Winter, Jay. "The Generation of Memory: Reflections on the 'Memory Boom' in Contemporary Historical Studies." *Bulletin of the German Historical Insitute* 27 (Fall 2000). May 7, 2006. http://www.ghi-dc.org/bulletin27F00/b27winter.html.

Zwinger, Lynda. "Blood Relations: Feminist Theory Meets the Uncanny Alien Bug Mother." *Hypatia* 7.2 (Spring 1992): 74–90.

Index

Elizabeth Ezra teaches French and global cinema at the University of Stirling, Scotland. She is the author of *Georges Méliès* and *The Colonial Unconscious,* editor of *European Cinema,* and coeditor of *France in Focus: Film and National Identity* and *Transnational Cinema: The Film Reader.*

Books in the series Contemporary Film Directors

Nelson Pereira dos Santos
  Darlene J. Sadlier

Abbas Kiarostami
  Mehrnaz Saeed-Vafa and
  Jonathan Rosenbaum

Joel and Ethan Coen
  R. Barton Palmer

Claire Denis
  Judith Mayne

Wong Kar-wai
  Peter Brunette

Edward Yang
  John Anderson

Pedro Almodóvar
  Marvin D'Lugo

Chris Marker
  Nora Alter

Abel Ferrara
  Nicole Brenez,
  translated by Adrian Martin

Jane Campion
  Kathleen McHugh

Jim Jarmusch
  Juan Suárez

Roman Polanski
  James Morrison

Manoel de Oliveira
  John Randal Johnson

Neil Jordan
  Maria Pramaggiore

Paul Schrader
  George Kouvaros

Jean-Pierre Jeunet
  Elizabeth Ezra